JOURNEY THROUGH THE BIBLE IN ELEVEN MONTHS

Copyright © 2023 by Carrie Carter

All rights reserved. No part of this book may be reproduced or copied in any form, by any means, electronic, mechanical, photocopying, recording, or by any information storage or retrieval system without prior written permission of the Publisher. Inquiries should be addressed to the name and email below.

The opinions expressed in this book are those solely of the author and do not reflect the opinions of Million Words Publishing or its Editors.

Scripture quotations are taken from KING JAMES VERSION (KJV): public domain.

Thank you.

Published By:
Million Words Publishing, LLC
Enjoyed By You!
WORDS THAT LAST FOREVER!®
www.millionwordspublishing.com
careemwp@att.net

Library of Congress Catalog Card Number:

ISBN #: 978-1-891282-30-0

Journey Through the Bible in Eleven Months
Printed in the United States of America

TABLE OF CONTENTS

Why Through the Bible in Eleven Months? 5
Reading Schedule 6-12
Weeks 1 – 2: Journey Through Genesis 13-15
Chapter One – This Can't Be My Life 16
Weeks 3 – 4: Journey Through Exodus 17-19
Chapter One – This Can't Be My Life (Cont.) 20
Week 5: Journey Through Leviticus 21-22
Chapter One – This Can't Be My Life (Cont.) 23
Weeks 6 – 7: Journey Through Numbers 24-26
Chapter Two – How Did I Get Here? 27
Weeks 8 – 9: Journey Through Deuteronomy 28-30
Chapter Three – The Worst Year 31
Week 10: Journey Through Joshua 32-33
Chapter Four – The Legacy 34
Week 11: Journey Through Judges 35-36
Week 11: Journey Through Ruth 37
He Led Me to a Clearing 38
Weeks 12 – 13: Journey Through 1 & 2 Samuel 39-41
There Were More Like Me 42
Weeks 14 – 15: Journey Through 1 & 2 Kings 43-45
Chapter Five – Passing on the Legacy 46
Weeks 16 – 18: Journey Through 1 & 2 Chronicles 47-50
Week 19: Journey Through Ezra 51-52
Week 19: Journey Through Nehemiah 53-54
Week 20: Journey Through Esther 55-56
Weeks 20 – 21: Journey Through Job 57-59
I Accept 60
Weeks 22 – 27: Journey Through Psalms 61-67
Week 28: Journey Through Proverbs 68-69
You Are My Father 70
Week 29: Journey Through Ecclesiastes 71-72
Week 29: Journey Through Song of Solomon 73-74

TABLE OF CONTENTS (Cont.)

Chapter Six – The Bad Day 75
Weeks 30 – 31: Journey Through Isaiah 76-78
Chapter Seven – The Bad Got Worse 79-80
Weeks 32 – 33: Journey Through Jeremiah 81-83
Chapter Eight – Could It Get Any Worse? 84
Week 33: Journey Through Lamentations 85-86
Weeks 34 – 35: Journey Through Ezekiel 87-89
I Say – You Say 90
Week 35: Journey Through Daniel 91-92
Week 36: Journey Through Hosea 93-94
Week 36: Journey Through Joel 95-96
Week 36: Journey Through Amos 97
Week 37: Journey Through Obadiah 98
Week 37: Journey Through Jonah 99-100
Week 37: Journey Through Micah 101-102
Week 37: Journey Through Nahum 103
Week 37: Journey Through Habakkuk 104-105
Week 37: Journey Through Zephaniah 106
Week 37: Journey Through Haggai 107
You Are Always Near 108
Week 38: Journey Through Zechariah 109-110
Week 38: Journey Through Malachi 111
Weeks 38 – 39: Journey Through Matthew 112-114
Weeks 39 – 40: Journey Through Mark 115-116
So Why Then Do We Pray? 117
Weeks 40 – 41: Journey Through Luke 118-120
Week 41: Journey Through John 121-123
Week 42: Journey Through Acts 124-126
Who Was Paul? 127
Week 43: Journey Through Romans 128-129
Week 43: Journey Through 1 Corinthians 130-131
Just a Sinner 132-133

TABLE OF CONTENTS (Cont.)

Week 44: Journey Through 2 Corinthians 134-135
My God Who Is Colorless 136
Week 44: Journey Through Galatians 137
Week 44: Journey Through Ephesians 138-139
Week 44: Journey Through Philippians 140
Week 45: Journey Through Colossians 141
Week 45: Journey Through 1 Thessalonians 142-143
Week 45: Journey Through 2 Thessalonians 144
Week 45: Journey Through 1 Timothy 145
Week 45: Journey Through 2 Timothy 146
Lisa Is Her Name 147
Week 46: Journey Through Titus 148
Week 46: Journey Through Philemon 149
Week 46: Journey Through Hebrews 150-151
Week 46: Journey Through James 152-153
Week 47: Journey Through 1 Peter 154
Week 47: Journey Through 2 Peter 155
Week 47: Journey Through 1 John 156-157
Week 47: Journey Through 2 John 158
Week 47: Journey Through 3 John 159
Week 47: Journey Through Jude 160
Week 48: Journey Through Revelation 161-163
I Am You and You Are Me 164-165
Answers 166-202
About the Author 203

WHY THROUGH THE BIBLE IN ELEVEN MONTHS?

As the Director of Christian Education at a church I once attended, one of my responsibilities and desires was to keep God's people in His Word. I believe that we all should read through the Bible once a year. I also love a challenge and wanted to challenge them with questions on what they were reading. Now, I had to figure out how to merge the two. So, I looked for a multifaceted study program. Unable to find exactly what I wanted, I decided, with much help from the Lord, along with some hard work, research, and determination to come up with a study program of my own. As a result, the quest to journey through the Bible in eleven months was conceived. I had many members to join and begin the journey with me, but only four people arrived at the destination. As the numbers dropped off, I was at first, a little disappointed. But God quickly and gently convicted and impressed on me, that if one person came to me for questions, I should be grateful. I soon realized that without these faithful few, I could not make this study, which is now my first book, *Journey Through the Bible in Eleven Months*, available to so many of you. In fact, if you start and finish this study, I sincerely believe you will be blessed.

As Christians, when the month of December arrives, we tend to get very busy. Extra time is taken for family and friends, and of course, the hustle and bustle of trying new recipes, attending parties, and finding the perfect gifts for those on our lists. However, this is the time of year that we should celebrate our Lord's birth. Yet, we so easily put our Bibles aside to "catch up" later with our reading of God's Word. This study is designed to take you through the Bible from Genesis to Revelation in eleven months. For some reason we all tend to want to start in the month of January, but this study can be started at any time of the year. So, I encourage you to just start whenever you want.

In addition, you will find intertwined my personal narratives and poems which I pray will provide you with insight, motivation, and encouragement along your journey. Also, there are questions to test your knowledge on what you've read. As you go through this study of God's Word, my prayer is that you not give up, and that He will open up to you the countless treasures that are found within the pages of the Bible. I am excited for you if this is your first time reading through the Bible, and I am excited for you if you have read through it before. God will truly bless each of us as we seek to better understand Him through His precious Word. So, let us start our *Journey Through the Bible in Eleven Months*.

READING SCHEDULE

This reading schedule is not, I repeat, is not, set in stone. It is setup for 48 weeks. However, this reading schedule is only a guide that you are free to alter to suit yourself. I recommend reading three to four chapters a day (sometimes more, sometimes less). Do only what is comfortable for you. You may get so caught up in the stories, that you want to keep going, and there will be days that you won't want to read at all. It is on those days that I encourage you to push through. This is where your blessing is revealed.

WEEK 1: GENESIS 1-25
DAY 1 - GENESIS 1-4
DAY 2 - GENESIS 5-8
DAY 3 - GENESIS 9-12
DAY 4 - GENESIS 13-16
DAY 5 - GENESIS 17-20
DAY 6 - GENESIS 21-25
DAY 7 REST, RELAX, REFLECT

WEEK 2: GENESIS 26-50
DAY 1 - GENESIS 26-29
DAY 2 - GENESIS 30-33
DAY 3 - GENESIS 34-37
DAY 4 - GENESIS 38-41
DAY 5 - GENESIS 42-45
DAY 6 - GENESIS 46-50
DAY 7 REST, RELAX, REFLECT

WEEK 3: EXODUS 1-20
DAY 1 - EXODUS 1-4
DAY 2 - EXODUS 5-7
DAY 3 - EXODUS 8-10
DAY 4 - EXODUS 11-14
DAY 5 - EXODUS 15-17
DAY 6 - EXODUS 18-20
DAY 7 REST, RELAX, REFLECT

WEEK 4: EXODUS 21-40
DAY 1 - EXODUS 21-24
DAY 2 - EXODUS 25-27
DAY 3 - EXODUS 28-31
DAY 4 - EXODUS 32-34
DAY 5 - EXODUS 35-37
DAY 6 - EXODUS 38-40
DAY 7 REST, RELAX, REFLECT

WEEK 5: LEVITICUS 1-27
DAY 1 - LEVITICUS 1-4
DAY 2 - LEVITICUS 5-9
DAY 3 - LEVITICUS 10-13
DAY 4 - LEVITICUS 14-18
DAY 5 - LEVITICUS 19-22
DAY 6 - LEVITICUS 23-27
DAY 7 REST, RELAX, REFLECT

WEEK 6: NUMBERS 1-18
DAY 1 - NUMBERS 1-3
DAY 2 - NUMBERS 4-6
DAY 3 - NUMBERS 7-9
DAY 4 - NUMBERS 10-12
DAY 5 - NUMBERS 13-15
DAY 6 - NUMBERS 16-18
DAY 7 REST, RELAX, REFLECT

READING SCHEDULE

WEEK 7: NUMBERS 19-36

DAY 1 - NUMBERS 19-21
DAY 2 - NUMBERS 22-24
DAY 3 - NUMBERS 25-27
DAY 4 - NUMBERS 28-30
DAY 5 - NUMBERS 31-33
DAY 6 - NUMBERS 34-36
DAY 7 REST, RELAX, REFLECT

WEEK 8: DEUTERONOMY 1-17

DAY 1 - DEUTERONOMY 1-3
DAY 2 - DEUTERONOMY 4-6
DAY 3 - DEUTERONOMY 7-8
DAY 4 - DEUTERONOMY 9-11
DAY 5 - DEUTERONOMY 12-14
DAY 6 - DEUTERONOMY 15-17
DAY 7 REST, RELAX, REFLECT

WEEK 9: DEUTERONOMY 18-34

DAY 1 - DEUTERONOMY 18-20
DAY 2 - DEUTERONOMY 21-22
DAY 3 - DEUTERONOMY 23-25
DAY 4 - DEUTERONOMY 26-28
DAY 5 - DEUTERONOMY 29-31
DAY 6 - DEUTERONOMY 32-34
DAY 7 REST, RELAX, REFLECT

WEEK 10: JOSHUA 1-24

DAY 1 - JOSHUA 1-4
DAY 2 - JOSHUA 5-8
DAY 3 - JOSHUA 9-12
DAY 4 - JOSHUA 13-16
DAY 5 - JOSHUA 17-20
DAY 6 - JOSHUA 21-24
DAY 7 REST, RELAX, REFLECT

WEEK 11: JUDGES 1-21; RUTH 1-4

DAY 1 - JUDGES 1-4
DAY 2 - JUDGES 5-8
DAY 3 - JUDGES 9-12
DAY 4 - JUDGES 13-16
DAY 5 - JUDGES 17-21
DAY 6 - RUTH 1-4
DAY 7 REST, RELAX, REFLECT

WEEK 12: 1 SAMUEL 1-31

DAY 1 - 1 SAMUEL 1-5
DAY 2 - 1 SAMUEL 6-10
DAY 3 - 1 SAMUEL 11-15
DAY 4 - 1 SAMUEL 16-21
DAY 5 - 1 SAMUEL 22-26
DAY 6 - 1 SAMUEL 27-31
DAY 7 REST, RELAX, REFLECT

WEEK 13: 2 SAMUEL 1-24

DAY 1 - 2 SAMUEL 1-4
DAY 2 - 2 SAMUEL 5-8
DAY 3 - 2 SAMUEL 9-12
DAY 4 - 2 SAMUEL 13-16
DAY 5 - 2 SAMUEL 17-20
DAY 6 - 2 SAMUEL 21-24
DAY 7 REST, RELAX, REFLECT

WEEK 14: 1 KINGS 1-22

DAY 1 - 1 KINGS 1-4
DAY 2 - 1 KINGS 5-8
DAY 3 - 1 KINGS 9-12
DAY 4 - 1 KINGS 13-16
DAY 5 - 1 KINGS 17-19
DAY 6 - 1 KINGS 20-22
DAY 7 REST, RELAX, REFLECT

READING SCHEDULE

WEEK 15: 2 KINGS 1-25

DAY 1 - 2 KINGS 1-4
DAY 2 - 2 KINGS 5-8
DAY 3 - 2 KINGS 9-12
DAY 4 - 2 KINGS 13-16
DAY 5 - 2 KINGS 17-21
DAY 6 - 2 KINGS 22-25
DAY 7 REST, RELAX, REFLECT

WEEK 16: 1 CHRONICLES 1-29

DAY 1 - 1 CHRONICLES 1-5
DAY 2 - 1 CHRONICLES 6-10
DAY 3 - 1 CHRONICLES 11-15
DAY 4 - 1 CHRONICLES 16-20
DAY 5 - 1 CHRONICLES 21-25
DAY 6 - 1 CHRONICLES 26-29
DAY 7 REST, RELAX, REFLECT

WEEK 17: 2 CHRONICLES 1-18

DAY 1 - 2 CHRONICLES 1-3
DAY 2 - 2 CHRONICLES 4-6
DAY 3 - 2 CHRONICLES 7-9
DAY 4 - 2 CHRONICLES 10-12
DAY 5 - 2 CHRONICLES 13-15
DAY 6 - 2 CHRONICLES 16-18
DAY 7 REST, RELAX, REFLECT

WEEK 18: 2 CHRONICLES 19-36

DAY 1 - 2 CHRONICLES 19-21
DAY 2 - 2 CHRONICLES 22-24
DAY 3 - 2 CHRONICLES 25-27
DAY 4 - 2 CHRONICLES 28-30
DAY 5 - 2 CHRONICLES 31-33
DAY 6 - 2 CHRONICLES 34-36
DAY 7 REST, RELAX, REFLECT

WEEK 19: EZRA 1-10; NEHEMIAH 1-13

DAY 1 - EZRA 1-3
DAY 2 - EZRA 4-6
DAY 3 - EZRA 7-10
DAY 4 - NEHEMIAH 1-4
DAY 5 - NEHEMIAH 5-8
DAY 6 - NEHEMIAH 9-13
DAY 7 REST, RELAX, REFLECT

WEEK 20: ESTHER 1-10; JOB 1-17

DAY 1 - ESTHER 1-5
DAY 2 - ESTHER 6-10
DAY 3 - JOB 1-4
DAY 4 - JOB 5-8
DAY 5 - JOB 9-13
DAY 6 - JOB 14-17
DAY 7 REST, RELAX, REFLECT

WEEK 21: JOB 18-42

DAY 1 - JOB 18-21
DAY 2 - JOB 22-25
DAY 3 - JOB 26-30
DAY 4 - JOB 31-34
DAY 5 - JOB 35-38
DAY 6 - JOB 39-42
DAY 7 REST, RELAX, REFLECT

WEEK 22: PSALMS 1-25

DAY 1 - PSALMS 1-4
DAY 2 - PSALMS 5-8
DAY 3 - PSALMS 9-13
DAY 4 - PSALMS 14-17
DAY 5 - PSALMS 18-21
DAY 6 - PSALMS 22-25
DAY 7 REST, RELAX, REFLECT

READING SCHEDULE

WEEK 23: PSALMS 26-50	**WEEK 24: PSALMS 51-75**
DAY 1 - PSALMS 26-29	DAY 1 - PSALMS 51-54
DAY 2 - PSALMS 30-33	DAY 2 - PSALMS 55-59
DAY 3 - PSALMS 34-37	DAY 3 - PSALMS 60-63
DAY 4 - PSALMS 38-42	DAY 4 - PSALMS 64-67
DAY 5 - PSALMS 43-46	DAY 5 - PSALMS 68-71
DAY 6 - PSALMS 47-50	DAY 6 - PSALMS 72-75
DAY 7 REST, RELAX, REFLECT	

WEEK 25: PSALMS 76-100	**WEEK 26: PSALMS 101-125**
DAY 1 - PSALMS 76-79	DAY 1 - PSALMS 101-105
DAY 2 - PSALMS 80-84	DAY 2 - PSALMS 106-110
DAY 3 - PSALMS 85-88	DAY 3 - PSALMS 111-114
DAY 4 - PSALMS 89-92	DAY 4 - PSALMS 115-118
DAY 5 - PSALMS 93-96	DAY 5 - PSALMS 119
DAY 6 - PSALMS 97-100	DAY 6 - PSALMS 120-125
DAY 7 REST, RELAX, REFLECT	

WEEK 27: PSALMS 126-150	**WEEK 28: PROVERBS 1-31**
DAY 1 - PSALMS 126-130	DAY 1 - PROVERBS 1-5
DAY 2 - PSALMS 131-134	DAY 2 - PROVERBS 6-10
DAY 3 - PSALMS 135-138	DAY 3 - PROVERBS 11-15
DAY 4 - PSALMS 139-142	DAY 4 - PROVERBS 16-20
DAY 5 - PSALMS 143-146	DAY 5 - PROVERBS 21-25
DAY 6 - PSALMS 147-150	DAY 6 - PROVERBS 26-31
DAY 7 REST, RELAX, REFLECT	

WEEK 29: ECCLESIASTES 1-12; SONG OF SOLOMON 1-8	**WEEK 30: ISAIAH 1-33**
DAY 1 - ECCLESIASTES 1-4	DAY 1 - ISAIAH 1-5
DAY 2 - ECCLESIASTES 5-7	DAY 2 - ISAIAH 6-10
DAY 3 - ECCLESIASTES 8-10	DAY 3 - ISAIAH 11-16
DAY 4 - ECCLESIASTES 11-12	DAY 4 - ISAIAH 17-22
DAY 5 - SONG OF SOLOMON 1-4	DAY 5 - ISAIAH 23-28
DAY 6 - SONG OF SOLOMON 5-8	DAY 6 - ISAIAH 29-33
DAY 7 REST, RELAX, REFLECT	

READING SCHEDULE

WEEK 31: ISAIAH 34-66	**WEEK 32: JEREMIAH 1-31**
DAY 1 - ISAIAH 34-38	DAY 1 - JEREMIAH 1-6
DAY 2 - ISAIAH 39-43	DAY 2 - JEREMIAH 7-11
DAY 3 - ISAIAH 44-48	DAY 3 - JEREMIAH 12-16
DAY 4 - ISAIAH 49-54	DAY 4 - JEREMIAH 17-22
DAY 5 - ISAIAH 55-60	DAY 5 - JEREMIAH 23-27
DAY 6 - ISAIAH 61-66	DAY 6 - JEREMIAH 28-31
DAY 7 REST, RELAX, REFLECT	

WEEK 33: JEREMIAH 32-52; LAMENTATIONS 1-5	**WEEK 34: EZEKIEL 1-30**
DAY 1 - JEREMIAH 32-35	DAY 1 - EZEKIEL 1-5
DAY 2 - JEREMIAH 36-39	DAY 2 - EZEKIEL 6-10
DAY 3 - JEREMIAH 40-43	DAY 3 - EZEKIEL 11-15
DAY 4 - JEREMIAH 44-47	DAY 4 - EZEKIEL 16-20
DAY 5 - JEREMIAH 48-52	DAY 5 - EZEKIEL 21-25
DAY 6 - LAMENTATIONS 1-5	DAY 6 - EZEKIEL 26-30
DAY 7 REST, RELAX, REFLECT	

WEEK 35: EZEKIEL 31-48; DANIEL 1-12	**WEEK 36: HOSEA 1-14; JOEL 1-3; AMOS 1-9**
DAY 1 - EZEKIEL 31-35	DAY 1 - HOSEA 1-4
DAY 2 - EZEKIEL 36-39	DAY 2 - HOSEA 5-9
DAY 3 - EZEKIEL 40-44	DAY 3 - HOSEA 10-14
DAY 4 - EZEKIEL 45-48	DAY 4 - JOEL 1-3
DAY 5 - DANIEL 1-6	DAY 5 - AMOS 1-4
DAY 6 - DANIEL 7-12	DAY 6 - AMOS 5-9
DAY 7 REST, RELAX, REFLECT	

READING SCHEDULE

WEEK 37: OBADIAH; JONAH 1-4; MICAH 1-7; NAHUM 1-3; HABAKKUK 1-3; ZEPHANIAH 1-3; HAGGAI 1-2

DAY 1 - OBADIAH; JONAH 1-4
DAY 2 - MICAH 1-7
DAY 3 - NAHUM 1-3
DAY 4 - HABAKKUK 1-3
DAY 5 - ZEPHANIAH 1-3
DAY 6 - HAGGAI 1-2
DAY 7 REST, RELAX, REFLECT

WEEK 38: ZECHARIAH 1-14; MALACHI 1-4; MATTHEW 1-10

DAY 1 - ZECHARIAH 1-5
DAY 2 - ZECHARIAH 6-10
DAY 3 - ZECHARIAH 11-14
DAY 4 - MALACHI 1-4
DAY 5 - MATTHEW 1-5
DAY 6 - MATTHEW 6-10
DAY 7 REST, RELAX, REFLECT

WEEK 39: MATTHEW 11-28; MARK 1-8

DAY 1 - MATTHEW 11-15
DAY 2 - MATTHEW 16-20
DAY 3 - MATTHEW 21-24
DAY 4 - MATTHEW 25-28
DAY 5 - MARK 1-4
DAY 6 - MARK 5-8
DAY 7 REST, RELAX, REFLECT

WEEK 40: MARK 9-16; LUKE 1-20

DAY 1 - MARK 9-12
DAY 2 - MARK 13-16
DAY 3 - LUKE 1-4
DAY 4 - LUKE 5-10
DAY 5 - LUKE 11-15
DAY 6 - LUKE 16-20
DAY 7 REST, RELAX, REFLECT

WEEK 41: LUKE 21-24; JOHN 1-21

DAY 1 - LUKE 21-24
DAY 2 - JOHN 1-4
DAY 3 - JOHN 5-9
DAY 4 - JOHN 10-14
DAY 5 - JOHN 15-18
DAY 6 - JOHN 19-21
DAY 7 REST, RELAX, REFLECT

WEEK 42: ACTS 1-28

DAY 1 - ACTS 1-4
DAY 2 - ACTS 5-9
DAY 3 - ACTS 10-14
DAY 4 - ACTS 15-19
DAY 5 - ACTS 20-24
DAY 6 - ACTS 25-28
DAY 7 REST, RELAX, REFLECT

READING SCHEDULE

WEEK 43: ROMANS 1-16; 1 CORINTHIANS 1-16	**WEEK 44: 2 CORINTHIANS 1-13; GALATIANS 1-6; EPHESIANS 1-6; PHILIPPIANS 1-4**
DAY 1 - ROMANS 1-5	DAY 1 - 2 CORINTHIANS 1-4
DAY 2 - ROMANS 6-10	DAY 2 - 2 CORINTHIANS 5-9
DAY 3 - ROMANS 11-16	DAY 3 - 2 CORINTHIANS 10-13
DAY 4 - 1 CORINTHIANS 1-5	DAY 4 - GALATIANS 1-6
DAY 5 - 1 CORINTHIANS 6-10	DAY 5 - EPHESIANS 1-6
DAY 6 - 1 CORINTHIANS 11-16	DAY 6 - PHILIPPIANS 1-4
DAY 7 REST, RELAX, REFLECT	

WEEK 45: COLOSSIANS 1-4; 1 THESSALONIANS 1-5; 2 THESSALONIANS 1-3; 1 TIMOTHY 1-6; 2 TIMOTHY 1-4	**WEEK 46: TITUS 1-3; PHILEMON; HEBREWS 1-13; JAMES 1-5**
DAY 1 - COLOSSIANS 1-4	DAY 1 - TITUS 1-3
DAY 2 - 1 THESSALONIANS 1-5	DAY 2 - PHILEMON
DAY 3 - 2 THESSALONIANS 1-3	DAY 3 - HEBREWS 1-5
DAY 4 - 1 TIMOTHY 1-3	DAY 4 - HEBREWS 6-9
DAY 5 - 1 TIMOTHY 4-6	DAY 5 - HEBREWS 10-13
DAY 6 - 2 TIMOTHY 1-4	DAY 6 - JAMES 1-5
DAY 7 REST, RELAX, REFLECT	

WEEK 47: 1 PETER 1-5; 2 PETER 1-3; 1 JOHN 1-5; 2 JOHN; 3 JOHN; JUDE	**WEEK 48: REVELATION 1-22**
DAY 1 - 1 PETER 1-5	DAY 1 - REVELATION 1-3
DAY 2 - 2 PETER 1-3	DAY 2 - REVELATION 4-7
DAY 3 - 1 JOHN 1-5	DAY 3 - REVELATION 8-10
DAY 4 - 2 JOHN	DAY 4 - REVELATION 11-14
DAY 5 - 3 JOHN	DAY 5 - REVELATION 15-18
DAY 6 - JUDE	DAY 6 - REVELATION 19-22
DAY 7 REST, RELAX, AND REFLECT ON A JOURNEY WELL DONE!	

Weeks 1 – 2: Journey Through Genesis

At the very beginning, we see God Himself as He speaks the world, as we know it, into existence. Here you get the very first glimpse of the Trinity. Try to imagine the scene as God forms man from the dust of the ground and breathes into him, the breath of life!

This is the start of your journey through the Bible. As you read the book of Genesis, you will find out how a rainbow came to be, and you may never look at one the same again. You will meet the patriarchs and see that they, like us, are only human. Pray for understanding, as you read about two great cities that God destroyed. You will discover the birth of twin boys—one that became the nation of Israel, and one that lost his birthright on an impulse. Do not feel sorry for Joseph, the dreamer, and his unfortunate events. God has a plan for him. As you walk through the pages of your Bible, I pray that you become hooked on the greatest story ever told!

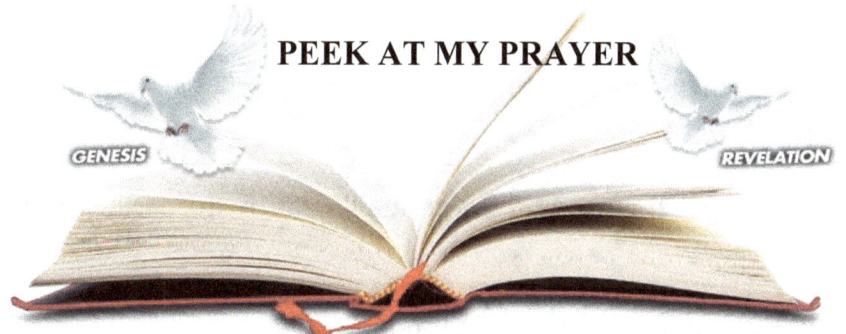

PEEK AT MY PRAYER

Father, thank You for those that choose to journey through this, Your Word. I pray that You will open our understanding and bless as only You can. Let us hear Your still, quiet voice in every Word that we read. Father, draw us near to Yourself. Please and thank You! In Jesus' name I pray. Amen!

Journey Through the Bible in Eleven Months

Questions Week 1 – Genesis Chapters 1-25

1. God created the heavens and the earth in six days. What was created each day and what happened on the seventh day? _____
   _____
   _____
   _____

2. Several times during creation, God saw that what He made was good. What did He see that was very good? _____

3. Where do we see marriage ordained by God? _____

4. Who were the first two sons of Adam and Eve? What were their jobs? _____
   _____

5. Who walked in close relationship with God and he was not, because God took him?
   _____

6. Why did God destroy the people and the earth? _____
   _____

7. What sign did God give that He would never again destroy the earth with water?
   _____

8. Who did God tell I will make of thee a great nation? _____

9. Abram was 99 when God changed his name. What did He change it to and why?
   _____

10. What was the outward sign of the covenant between Abraham and God? _____
    _____

11. Who did God refer to as Abraham's only son? _____

12. What was Isaac's wife's name, and what were the names of their twin sons? _____
    _____
    _____

Journey Through Genesis

Questions Week 2 – Genesis Chapters 26-50

1. Jacob conspired with his mother to lie to his father Isaac. Why? _____

2. When Esau considered killing his brother Jacob, where did his mother send him? _____

3. What are the names of the daughters of Laban that Jacob eventually married? _____

4. How did Laban trick Jacob? _____

5. How did Rachel die, and what were the names of her two sons? _____

6. Who was the favorite son of Jacob (Israel) and what gift did Jacob give to him? _____

7. When the sons of Jacob (Israel) conspired to kill the favorite son, how was he saved? _____

8. When the brothers went to Egypt the second time to get food, who were they to bring with them? _____

9. Who are the 12 sons/tribes of Jacob (Israel)? _____

    Extra Credit: Which tribal line did Jesus come from? _____

Chapter One – This Can't Be My Life

They were eight, nine, and ten; two boys and a girl. The girl was the oldest. Their mother asked the youngest where the other two were, but he didn't know. She went back in the apartment wanting a cigarette bad, but she had none. The night before was the reason why. She had spent every dime getting high. She walked into the kitchen and opened the refrigerator, nothing there. She opened the cabinets, nothing there but a can of corn. What was she going to feed them? As she turned to leave the kitchen, her youngest stood in the doorway. He wouldn't leave her side, almost as if she would disappear if he couldn't see her. She asked him again where his brother and sister were. He just shrugged his little shoulders and said he didn't know. Hours later, as it began to get dark, she began to worry about her children. She knew that she wasn't a very good mother, but she loved her children very much. *Please God, let them be alright*, she thought as she went to look for them. She called their names, no answer. She called louder, still no answer. Fear had settled in her heart as she started toward her car—a car with little to no gas in it. Where were they? The streetlights were on, but no children. As she started the car, she saw them walking side by side, a paper bag in the hand of her daughter. As she got out of the car, they saw her and began to run toward her crying out, "Mommy! Mommy! Look what we got. Look what we got!" There was excitement in their little eyes and in their little voices. They were proud of their accomplishment and eager to share it with her . . .

Weeks 3 – 4: Journey Through Exodus

When we begin the book of Exodus, all of the generation of Israel including his sons have died. The new Pharaoh does not care for this people who have multiplied greatly and become powerful. He forces them into slavery, and they have begun to cry out to God. A baby boy named Moses arrives on the scene and he will be the man to lead God's people out of bondage from a place called Egypt.

You will see God warn this king with supernatural plagues. You will see how the Passover came to be. You will stand on the banks of the Red Sea and watch as God parts it, so that His people could walk through on dry ground.

Listen as the people complain after their deliverance. Go up to Mt. Sinai with Moses as he receives the Ten Commandments, written by God Himself. Instructions for the tabernacle and where the Ark of the Covenant will be, are given. Then stand with God's people as He dwells among them.

PEEK AT MY PRAYER

Father, thank You so much for those that have made it this far. Bless them as only You can. Walk with them through every moment of their lives. Please and thank You! In Jesus' name I pray. Amen!

Journey Through the Bible in Eleven Months

Questions Week 3 – Exodus Chapters 1-20

1. When Pharaoh's daughter found a baby in the river, who did she pay to feed him?

2. What did she name the baby and what is the meaning of the name?

3. When Moses asks God what he should tell the people when they ask who sent him, what does God tell him to say?

4. From what tribe are Aaron and Moses?

5. What are the 10 plagues that God brought upon Egypt?

6. What saved the children of Israel from the plague of the death of the first-born? In your own words, explain this.

7. How did the LORD divide the Red Sea?

8. Who was the sister of Moses and Aaron?

9. Who was Moses' father-in-law and how did he help Moses?

10. Why do you think that the first four commandments are so important?

11. What is the first commandment with promise?

Journey Through Exodus

Questions Week 4 – Exodus Chapters 21-40

1. The LORD told the people three times they shall keep a feast unto Him in the year. Name these feasts. _____
   _____
   _____

2. How long was Moses up on Mt. Sinai with God? _____
   _____

3. The Ark of the Covenant was overlaid with what precious metal? _____
   _____

4. Where did the veil (curtain) hang in the tabernacle? _____
   _____

5. Who wrote the Ten Commandments? _____

6. Why did Moses break the stone tablets of the Ten Commandments? _____
   _____
   _____

7. What part of God did Moses see? _____

8. How did God guide the children of Israel through the wilderness? _____
   _____
   _____

Journey Through the Bible in Eleven Months

Chapter One – This Can't Be My Life (Cont.)

. . . She looked at her children and just could not stop the shaking. Her mind had gotten away from her, and she had thought the worst. "I was so worried about you, where have you been?" she asked them. They were excited, so excited that they could not be still. "We were at the market, and, and, and this lady was walking to her car." Her son joined in, "She dropped all her stuff; her bags just broke. Three bags just broke open, and all her stuff was all over the ground." They were taking turns telling the story. Her head went back and forth as they competed with each other to tell her what had happened. "And nobody was helping her, so we did. We picked up all her stuff, and we put it in her car. She was old," they told her. "How old was she?" she asked as her anxiety began to fade. "She was old like you." This brought a smile to her face. "Oh, man," she said. "Old like me, huh?" They were eager to tell the rest of the story. "Yeah, like you mommy, and she gave us some money, and then we were asking people if they needed help, and we were just helping everybody, and everybody gave us money." Back and forth they told her where they had been. She was just relieved that they were alright.

"Look what we bought! Look what we bought!" They shouted as they handed her their prize. She took the little brown bag, and as she opened it, they danced around her. They were happy to share, and so proud of themselves. As she looked in the bag, they stopped dancing when they saw the tears on her face. They thought that she would be happy, and were confused by the tears. . . .

Week 5: Journey Through Leviticus

The book of Leviticus picks up right where Exodus ends. God reveals His laws and commands to Moses, who then passes them on to the Israelites. You will see the many different offerings, how they were made, why they were made, and instructions for how to approach the Holiness of God, with the help of the priest, by sinful people. The laws were given as a guide to worshipping our Holy God and to show man that they were sinful. The priests were held to a higher standard because they were to go to God on behalf of the people. You will also see the different festivals that were to be celebrated each year.

Moses is still the man that God told everything to, and he in turn told the people. He also wrote down everything that God told him, as he is the man that wrote this book also.

PEEK AT MY PRAYER

Father, thank You again, for those that have made it to this destination. Give each one of them the understanding that You want them to have. I know that Your love for them is great. Let them feel this love as they continue their journey through Your Word. Please and thank You! In Jesus' name I pray. Amen!

Journey Through the Bible in Eleven Months

Questions Week 5 – Leviticus Chapters 1-27

1. If the whole congregation of Israel sinned through ignorance, what was their offering to be? _____

   _____

2. How long were the priests told to stay in the tabernacle of the congregation to be consecrated? _____

3. Two of Aaron's sons sinned against God. What were their names, and what happened to them? _____

   _____

   _____

   _____

4. After childbirth, how long was a woman considered to be unclean? _____

   _____

5. Why did God tell Moses to tell the Israelites to be holy? _____

   _____

   _____

6. Name two different feasts that the children of Israel were commanded to keep. _____

   _____

   _____

   _____

7. To whom did God give all of the commandments and where did this take place? _____

   _____

   _____

Chapter One – This Can't Be My Life (Cont.)

... The tears just seemed to keep coming and coming, and her children just kept staring and frowning. They had believed and thought she would be happy. They looked as if they were going to cry. "Mommy, what's the matter?" They asked. She tried to pull it together, but she couldn't. She looked in the bag again, and all she could do was gather her children in her arms and cry onto their tiny shoulders. *Hell No!* Her mind screamed. *Hell No, my kids are taking care of me when I'm supposed to be taking care of them. HELL NO, HELL NO, HELL NO! Oh God, this can't be my life. This can't be my life.*

"We're sorry Mommy," her daughter said with confusion all over her small face. "No baby, I'm not mad at you. You didn't do anything wrong," and as she wiped the tears and snot off of her face, she opened that small brown bag, and looked inside again. Inside that small brown bag was a pack of hot dogs, a pack of hot dog buns, and a pack of cigarettes. Her children were taking care of her.

Journey Through the Bible in Eleven Months

Weeks 6 – 7: Journey Through Numbers

A little over a year after leaving Egypt, God told Moses to take a census, or numbering, of all the men 20 years old and older who were able to serve in the army. The Levites were not numbered, as they were the priests and were set aside for the work of the Lord.

The blessing of the Promised Land is so very close, but the people complain and seem not to fully trust God. As a consequence, they wander for 40 years. You will meet Caleb and Joshua, two men who dared to go against the majority, and how God blessed them.

You will see many try to rebel against Moses - leaders, priests, even his own brother and sister. But God was the one in control and was the shield for Moses.

You will understand that Moses is a prayer warrior, as he intercedes for the people, over and over, and over again (never stop praying) and compassion will overwhelm you as you listen to God tell him that he would not go into the Promised Land.

PEEK AT MY PRAYER

Thank You, Father, for the hearts that continue this journey. Teach them as they read and meditate on Your most holy and mighty Word. Please and thank You! In Jesus' name I pray. Amen!

Journey Through Numbers

Questions Week 6 – Numbers Chapters 1-18

1. Why did God call for a census of all the men 20 years and older? _____

2. Why weren't the Levites numbered with the tribes to be able to fight? _____

3. When a person took a special vow of a Nazarite to separate themselves to the LORD, what were they not to do? _____

4. At what age were the Levites to begin their service in the tabernacle and at what age were they to retire? _____

5. What stopped the LORD's anger when the people complained about their hardship? _____

6. When the people complained of no meat, what did God make fall all around the camp? _____

7. What happened to Miriam when she complained about Moses being married to an Ethiopian woman? _____

8. Twelve spies were sent into Canaan to search out the land. How many came back with a good report? Who were they? _____

9. Who led a revolt against Moses and Aaron, and what happened to them? _____

10. When 12 rods were taken into the tabernacle, one rod changed. Who did it belong to and how did it change? _____

Journey Through the Bible in Eleven Months

Questions Week 7 – Numbers Chapters 19-36

1. What was the sin of Moses and the consequences of it? _____
   _____
   _____

2. When Israel sinned by committing whoredoms, and worshipping Baal-peor, who turned the wrath of God away from them and was given the promise of peace? _____
   _____
   _____

3. Who was appointed as the successor to Moses? _____

4. When Israel went to war with the Midianites, who were they told not to kill? _____
   _____

5. How old was Aaron when he died? _____

6. What was the Promised Land? _____
   _____

7. When there was no male heir, how did the women inherit their father's land? _____
   _____
   _____

Chapter Two – How Did I Get Here?

She, her husband, and children had just gotten their place in the bad part of town. It seemed alright in the daytime, but it came alive at night, and that was fine with her. She was in her element. She knew where to go, and who to see to get high. When it came to drugs, her motto was, "Where there's a will, there's a way." She set out every day to get high.

They had been staying with her brother and sister-in-law. As they were preparing to move into their place, her husband went to score, and came back with no money. Someone had stolen his wallet with their life savings (of $600.00) in it. She was so angry that she considered hitting him. Her anger gave way to hurt, and then the tears started. She laid down on the bed and cried and cried until no more tears would come.

"Oh God," she cried out. "How did I get here? Oh God, Oh God, Oh God, please help me. Please help me." From the deepest part of her, she cried out to a God that she didn't know. She was praying and didn't even know it. All of a sudden, she felt something roll through her entire body. It scared her so bad that she sat straight up in the bed and said, "No."

It was at that very moment in her life, that she became His; a God that loved her had just claimed her as His own. She had just been sealed by the Holy Ghost.

Journey Through the Bible in Eleven Months

Weeks 8 – 9: Journey Through Deuteronomy

After leaving Egypt, God's people have been in the wilderness for 40 years. This is a new generation, a generation that was not present at the beginning. Therefore, they did not witness the parting of the Red Sea, nor were they present at the giving of the law.

Moses feels the need to remind them of the mighty God that loves them. He will go over their history before they go into the Promised Land. He was their leader for so long that it is on his heart to refresh them. He wants them to do right. He loves them so much!

This Moses, this man of miracles, knows that his time is short. He really wants them to understand who they are and who they belong to. He is preaching to them and he is teaching them with high expectations. Time and time again, he has gone on his knees for them.

What a life this man lived! But because these people that he loved so much angered him to the point of disobeying God, he was not going to go into the Promised Land. God told him that he was going to "rest with your fathers," but that the people would forsake him and break the covenant he had made with them. Moses did see the land that had been promised, but he was not able to possess it.

PEEK AT MY PRAYER

Father, thank You for Your Word. Help us to always keep it in our hearts. Teach us Lord. Please and thank You! In Jesus' name I pray. Amen!

Journey Through Deuteronomy

Questions Week 8 – Deuteronomy Chapters 1-17

1. When Moses told the people you are as the stars of heaven, what did he want for them?

2. Why was Caleb able to go into the Promised Land?

3. How did the people hear the voice of God?

4. Finish this sentence: Man does not live by bread alone, _____

5. Moses was so angry with the sin of the people that he broke the two tablets of the covenant. Then what did he do?

6. When a prophet tried to entice a child of Israel into following other gods, what was his punishment?

7. What was the month that the Hebrews were told to observe always and why?

8. What happened to anyone caught serving other gods?

Journey Through the Bible in Eleven Months

Questions Week 9 – Deuteronomy Chapters 18-34

1. What was the inheritance of the Levites? _____
_____
_____

2. When a man had taken a new wife, how long was he free from going to war, to take care of business and cheer up his wife? _____
_____

3. What was the year of tithing? _____

4. During the 40 years of wandering, what never got worn out? _____
_____

5. Where were the Levites told to put the book of the law? _____
_____
_____

6. On what mountain did Moses go up to to die? _____

7. How old was Moses when he died? _____
_____

8. How long did the children of Israel mourn and weep for Moses? _____
_____

9. Which books of the Bible did Moses write? _____
_____
_____

Chapter Three – The Worst Year

The next year was not a very good one. In fact, it was the worst year of her life. She wished that she could say that after the spirit of God took possession of her, that she did everything right, but she didn't. She still set out to get high every day, and still wasn't a very good mother. She wished that she could tell you that her life was different, but it wasn't; it seemed to be worse. You see, she had prayed in her despair. God heard her, and claimed her by sealing her with His Spirit. She just didn't know it, and there began to be a struggle within her. On the one hand, she wanted to continue her life as it was, but on the other, something inside of her, deep down inside of her, wanted to do right.

One day as she was sitting at her buddy's house, (who was not her friend, but her let's get high buddy, her ride or die buddy, and whatever way the wind blows buddy) something happened. They were passing the pipe back and forth, back and forth, when as she held the smoke in, tears began to roll down her cheeks, and she couldn't stop them. Soon she was crying, full-fledged crying. As her buddy took the pipe, she looked at her like she was crazy with a question in her eyes, but the tears wouldn't stop. She couldn't have stopped them if she wanted to and as she reached for the pipe, hit it, held the smoke in, she looked her buddy right in the eye, and as the smoke left her body, she said, "This can't be my life."

Week 10: Journey Through Joshua

After the death of Moses, God chooses Joshua to lead the children of Israel. Joshua was very close to Moses; he may have been a personal assistant. God tells him to be strong and courageous, and to be careful to obey all of the law.

Between the people and the Promised Land flows the Jordan River. Through Joshua God will stop the flow so that the people can cross over it. On that day, Joshua was exalted by God. The people revered him as they had Moses.

You will learn that he is a mighty warrior with much faith. God will use Joshua to bring down the mighty walls of Jericho, and He will guide him through every battle to capture the Promised Land.

Joshua was well liked and respected by the children of Israel. Joshua is the one who said, "Choose you this day, whom you shall serve, and as for me and my house, we will serve the Lord."

PEEK AT MY PRAYER

Thank You, Father, for the opportunity to learn about a man of such great faith. Please help us to see ourselves as we study Your Word. With each word that is read, Father, please bless like only You can. Thank You for each person who will learn more about You. In Jesus' name I pray. Amen!

Journey Through Joshua

Questions Week 10 – Joshua Chapters 1-24

1. Who was the harlot that hid the two spies in Jericho? _____

2. What did she ask of these two spies? _____
   _____

3. How did the children of Israel cross the Jordan River without drowning? _____
   _____

4. When did the manna stop appearing? _____
   _____

5. Joshua saw a man with his sword drawn. Who was he and what did he tell Joshua?
   _____
   _____

6. How many times were the men of war to march around the city of Jericho and what happened on the last day? _____
   _____
   _____

7. Joshua asked that the _____ and _____ stand still. How long did they stand still? _____

8. How many kings did the children of Israel defeat in the Promised Land? _____

9. What portion of land did Caleb inherit and why? _____
   _____
   _____

10. What were the cities of refuge designated for? _____
    _____
    _____

11. Why did the tribes of Reuben, Gad, and the half tribe of Manasseh build a replica of the LORD's altar? _____
    _____
    _____

Chapter Four – The Legacy

And it wasn't her life. She had a legacy that she could not deny. Growing up she had a grandmother (fondly called Memaw) that her family visited often. Her home was in another state, and anytime that they went, there was always excitement. Memaw's house was tiny, but overflowing with much love. The small girl loved sleeping under the dining room table; she could hear the TV, and she could hear the grownups as they laughed and talked about the olden days.

One of her favorite parts of visiting Memaw's house was waking to the sound of the creaking of the narrow stairs as her grandmother made her way down from her bed in the attic. It was always early, and the girl always pretended to be asleep. The stairs ended right there in the dining room. This is where Memaw would pull a chair out from under the table, get down on her knees in front of that chair, put her hands together, bow her head, and close her eyes. This is when she would open hers and watch this Matriarch as her lips began to move, and tears seemed to always slip from her eyes. Peace unseen, but very evident even to the young girl, always settled over her. She was mesmerized as she heard whispers to God. Memaw would pray for what seemed like a long time, but only because she mentioned everybody's name. The girl got a happy overwhelming feeling in her heart when she heard her own name. Memaw was talking to God about her. She didn't understand it then at eight years old, but she would, 25 years later, when she gave her life to that same God that her grandmother had talked to every morning. She now understood that somebody had loved her so much that they prayed for her; got down on their knees for her, and cried out to God for her. She also understood that even though Memaw didn't see her saved, didn't see her give her life to the Lord, didn't see her loving Him, and didn't see her as she too got down on her knees for her own grandchildren. This woman of faith had left a legacy that she could not deny, a rich, overwhelming legacy for her to carry on.

Week 11: Journey Through Judges

After the death of Joshua, the nation of Israel does not have a leader. Therefore, they do not continue with their conquest of the land that God had promised them. They turned from God and began to worship idols. In short, they were content with their lives and did what they wanted.

So, God chose mighty people to be the judges and leaders for His people. They would do good as long as someone was leading them. Once a judge died, they again went right back to their disobedience.

You will meet the judges that were handpicked by God. Some are just mentioned with no record of what they did. But others are recorded in depth. Samson is probably the most famous of the judges because of his downfall by a woman named Delilah. He was one of the last judges before God appointed kings to lead his people.

Dear God, I just cannot thank You enough for these, Your people. As they learn more about You, I pray that You would draw them closer to You. Please and thank You! In Jesus' name I pray. Amen!

Journey Through the Bible in Eleven Months

Questions Week 11 – Judges Chapters 1-21

1. How did the first judge come to be? What was his name? _____
   _____
   _____

2. Who was the judge who sent and called Barak? What was unique about this judge?
   _____
   _____
   _____

3. God told Gideon that he would defeat the Midianites, but that he had too many men. How many men did he start and end with? _____
   _____

4. What was the rash vow Jephthah made to the LORD for victory over the children of Ammon, and what did this vow cost him? _____
   _____
   _____
   _____
   _____

5. Which judge was a Nazarite from his mother's womb? _____
6. Who was the cause of his downfall? _____
7. Why was there war between the nation of Israel and the tribe of Benjamin? _____
   _____
   _____
   _____

Week 11: Journey Through Ruth

In the book of Ruth, you will meet a woman who dedicated herself to her mother-in-law, Naomi, and the God that she served. Naomi, at this time, has lost her husband and both of her sons. She is heartbroken and just wants to go back home to Judah. Also, she hears that the Lord has come to the aid of his people, by providing them with food.

As Naomi urges both of her daughters-in-law to go and live their lives, Ruth is determined to stay with her. She vowed that only death would separate them. The love that Ruth has toward her mother-in-law is strong. These two women show us by their faithfulness to God and each other, that even when times are hard, God has a plan.

PEEK AT MY PRAYER

Lord God Almighty, You are wonderful beyond measure. I love You and thank You for this example of who You are and what You can do with a willing heart. Continue to bless the hearts of Your people. Please and thank You! In Jesus' name I pray. Amen!

✝✝✝✝✝✝✝✝✝✝✝✝✝✝✝✝✝✝✝✝✝✝✝✝✝✝✝✝✝✝✝✝✝✝✝✝✝✝✝

Questions Week 11 – Ruth Chapters 1-4

1. What were the names of Naomi's daughters-in-law? _____
2. Why did Naomi let Ruth stay with her? _____
   _____
3. Who was the kinsman redeemer that married Ruth? _____
4. Who was their child and who was he the grandfather of? _____
   _____

Journey Through the Bible in Eleven Months

HE LED ME TO A CLEARING

I was in a wood that was dark and dense,
I kept hearing my name and could make no sense.

When I heard my name, I couldn't turn around.
I kept on trying, but I got pushed to the ground.

There was darkness in my mind, and darkness in my soul.
Was I in a play with someone choosing my role?

And still I heard my name in that dark, lonely place.
The briars and the thorns kept touching my face.

There was weakness and pain and there was sadness too,
Then I heard His voice, "Child **I AM** here to help you."

I knew who He was, but I asked, "Are you real?"
He took my hand, and my heart started to heal.

He led me to a clearing at the edge of the wood.
It was so beautiful and bright and I knew it was good.

He said, "Step over my child, for now is the time.
Do not hesitate; you must cross over the line."

The grass was so green and the flowers so bright.
I felt in my soul that this place, it was right.

"**I AM** with you always," said that wonderful voice.
I knew that He would; I had made the right choice.

I stepped into the light and suddenly felt warm.
I was the reason that He had been born.

Weeks 12 – 13: Journey Through 1 & 2 Samuel

In these two books, you will see the transition from judges to kings. Samuel was the last man to judge over Israel. His mother Hannah, who was barren, prayed for a child, and when he was born, she dedicated him to the Lord. He grows up in the temple and is truly a man of God. Not only was he a mighty judge, but he was also a prophet and a priest.

He will anoint Saul, the first king of Israel and will hold him accountable to the God that he serves. When Saul disobeys the Word of God, Samuel is sent to anoint the second king of Israel, David. Samuel loves the people of Israel and wants with his whole heart for them to turn back to the true and living God.

These two books are one continuous story with the first book focusing on Samuel, Saul, and David. The second book focuses on David and his victories and failures. Samuel lived his life to please God, and he dies (in the first book) having done all that God asks of him.

Father God, You and You alone are worthy of all our praise. Thank You for the life of Samuel and may we strive to be like him in our lives. Please and thank You! In Jesus' name I pray. Amen!

Journey Through the Bible in Eleven Months

Questions Week 12 – 1 Samuel Chapters 1-31

1. Who was Samuel's mother? _____

2. How many times did the LORD call Samuel before he answered Him? _____

3. Why did the wife of Phinehas name her child Ichabod? _____
   _____

4. Who did Samuel anoint as the first king of Israel? _____

5. Why was this king rejected by God? _____
   _____

6. Who did Samuel anoint as the second king of Israel? _____
   _____

7. Why was Saul afraid of David? _____
   _____

8. What did David do to Saul to prove to him that he could have killed him? _____
   _____
   _____

9. Who saved Nabal and his whole household from being killed by David? _____
   _____

10. How does Saul's life end? _____
    _____
    _____

Journey Through 2 Samuel

Questions Week 13 – 2 Samuel Chapters 1-24

1. How did David and his men react to the death of Saul and his son, Jonathan?

2. Jonathan had a son who was lame in both feet. How did he become lame, and what was his name?

3. Why do you think that Uzzah was struck down by the LORD?

4. When David first sees Bathsheba, he was home in the palace. Where should he have been?

5. Why did David try to trick Uriah, Bathsheba's husband, and why didn't it work?

6. When David couldn't trick Uriah, what did he order done to him?

7. What happened to the first son born to David and Bathsheba?

8. What was the name of their second son?

9. What happened to David's son, Amnon, after he forced his sister Tamar to lie with him?

10. What was Absalom's goal in his adult life?

11. How did Absalom die?

Journey Through the Bible in Eleven Months

THERE WERE MORE LIKE ME

When He found me, I was face down in the dirt.
He picked me up gently by the scruff of my shirt.

His hands wiped the grime off of my face.
"You belong to me; I'll show you your place."

He cut away what I thought I would need.
I knew that any moment I'd start to bleed.

He broke me and turned me every which way.
I tried to be still, but I started to sway.

"Be still little one and just look around."
I saw more like me with their faces in the ground.

"Can't you see that there is work to be done?
There are others like you who need to be won."

I looked to the left, and I looked to the right.
He was molding me to go out and fight.

It hurt, and it hurt, and it hurt some more,
But nothing like the pain that He'd already bore.

He was the Master determined to fit me in His hand.
I say, "I can't do this." He says, "Child, yes you can."

"When I tell you to speak, there'll be someone to hear,
And remember I'm with you, I'll always be near."

I thought I was ready, but I started to tire.
He said, "One more step, you must go through the fire."

"And when you come out, you'll be as pure gold.
You don't even know it, but for me you'll be bold."

Just a little longer my child, I am almost done.
When I am finished with you, this race you will run.

And when I came through, I couldn't see me,
But now I was who I was supposed to be.

I stood up straight and I stood up tall.
I knew on my life He had placed a call.

"I see that you are ready to enter the war.
You will get battered, be bruised, and be sore."

"You now are an instrument that I'm ready to use.
Go put on your armor and tie up your shoes!"

Weeks 14 – 15: Journey Through 1 & 2 Kings

These two books are exactly what they are titled, about the kings that ruled over Israel and Judah. When the kingdom split there were always two kings ruling. The book of 1 Kings opens with the death of David and the ascension of Solomon as the third king over Israel. After his death, the kingdom becomes divided. There were some kings that did evil in the sight of God; there were some that did right in the sight of God, and then there were a few who were zealous and really wanted to please only God.

You will meet two exceptional prophets, Elijah and Elisha. Elijah dared to confront evil and at times thought that he was the only one that served God. He passes his mantle on to Elisha, who asked for a double portion of what Elijah had. God used them mightily. These two men were miracle workers used by God because of their faith and trust in Him.

Dear God, thank You for making Your Word come alive to us. We see the same kinds of people in our world today. Help each of us strive to be exceptional in Your sight. Please and thank You! In Jesus' name I pray. Amen!

Journey Through the Bible in Eleven Months

Questions Week 14 – 1 Kings Chapters 1-22

1. Which of David's sons tried to make himself king when David was old and close to death?

2. Who became king after David died? _____

3. How long did David reign as king of Israel? _____

4. What gift does Solomon ask for when God offers him anything he wants? _____

5. Why was Solomon able to build the house of the LORD when David was not? _____

6. How long did it take Solomon to build the house? How long did it take him to build his palace? _____

7. Who came from a far distance to test Solomon's wisdom? _____

8. How many wives and concubines did Solomon have and why was this dangerous?

9. Which king did more evil than any king before him and who was his wife? _____

10. How many false prophets did Elijah tell Ahab to gather? _____

11. Who did Elijah cast his mantle upon (pass his legacy to)? _____

12. Why did Ahaziah, the son of Ahab, reign only two years over Israel? _____

Journey Through 2 Kings

Questions Week 15 – 2 Kings Chapters 1-25

1. How did Elijah die? _____
   _____
   _____

2. How did Elisha help the poor widow? _____
   _____
   _____

3. What did God allow the servant of Elisha to see when they were surrounded by the enemy? _____
   _____

4. Which king had the 70 sons of Ahab beheaded, the family of Ahaziah killed, and the worshippers of Baal killed? _____

5. How did Jezebel die? _____
   _____

6. When the LORD was angry with Israel, who did He allow to take them into captivity?
   _____

7. Which king did that which was right, just as David, his father, had done? _____
   _____

8. When he prayed to the LORD, how many years did God add to Hezekiah's life? _____

9. Who began to rule and became king at a very young age, and turned to the LORD with all his heart, with all his soul, and with all his might? _____

Chapter Five – Passing on the Legacy

Two of her nieces and her oldest grandson were visiting for the summer. She made it her priority to get up early, while the house was still quiet. This was her time to spend with the Lord. She made her way down the hall to her living room and stopped in front of the couch. She knelt down, folded her hands under her chin, bowed her head, and closed her eyes. As she spoke the words, "Good Morning Father," she felt movement beside her. She opened her eyes and there next to her was her seven-year-old grandson. He was on his knees, hands folded under his chin, his head was bowed, and his eyes were closed. She was caught off guard, but pure joy overwhelmed her. "Do you want to pray with me?" He nodded his head once. "Do you want to talk to the Lord, or do you want me to?" she asked. With his hands still clasped beneath his chin, he pointed one little finger toward her. He never opened his eyes. Her heart was humbled as she spoke to the Lord with this little guy beside her. She made sure that he heard his name being spoken to the Lord.

She would never forget that day and prayed that he would always remember. Today, as a young man serving his country, he makes time to call her, and often their conversations last an hour or more. Sometimes he asks that she pray for him, and other times, he lets her know what the Lord is doing in his life. "Hey Grandma, will you pray for me?" "I sure will," she replies. "Hey Grandma, guess what God did?" "I know it's good," she says with a smile in her heart. He replies, "I love you Grandma." And after every call, she bows her head and says, "Thank You Father."

Weeks 16 – 18: Journey Through 1 & 2 Chronicles

The books of the Chronicles are a recap of everything from the genealogy of the children of Israel, to the kings, to the captivity, to the decree by Cyrus allowing them to go back home. First Chronicles takes us from Adam to Solomon ascending to the throne. Second Chronicles goes into the reign of the kings of Judah.

As you work your way through these two books, you will recognize some of the people, and some you will not. You will meet some evil kings, some good kings, and then you will meet some great kings. These great kings wanted only to please God and not man. They had their faults as we all do; but watch God in their lives.

When one king died, there was always another to take his place. Moreover, according to how a king led, that was how the people lived their lives. The children of Israel were wishy-washy. They did badly. God would punish them, and then they would do well. He allowed them to go into captivity for 70 years and then He let them go back home.

Hello Father. Lord, as we study Your Word, let us see who we are to You. Help us to lean and depend on You for everything. We need You in this world that we live in today. And we will love You always. Please and thank You! In Jesus' name I pray. Amen!

Journey Through the Bible in Eleven Months

Questions Week 16 – 1 Chronicles Chapters 1-29

1. Who was the first man? _____

2. Who were the eight people on the ark? _____
   _____

3. Name the 12 sons of Israel. _____
   _____
   _____

4. Why did Saul die? _____
   _____

5. Who did David say could carry the ark of God, and why? _____
   _____

6. At the celebration of the ark coming to the city of David, what did David give to every man and woman? _____
   _____

7. David angered God when he numbered the people. What were the consequences?
   _____
   _____

8. Who became king after David? _____

9. Who were the Levites and what were their jobs? _____
   _____
   _____
   _____

10. Why wouldn't God let David build a new place for Him to dwell in? _____
    _____
    _____

Journey Through 2 Chronicles

Questions Week 17 – 2 Chronicles Chapters 1-18

1. What was the gift that God gave to Solomon? _____

2. Where was the house of the LORD built? _____

3. Where did God (the Ark of the Covenant) dwell in the house? _____

4. What did God tell His people to do, in order for Him to heal the land? _____

5. Why did the Queen of Sheba come to Jerusalem? _____

6. How long did Solomon reign over Israel? _____

7. Who was the son of Abijah that did what was right in the sight of the LORD? _____

8. How did the prophet Azariah encourage Asa? _____

Journey Through the Bible in Eleven Months

Questions Week 18 – 2 Chronicles Chapters 19-36

1. What did the son of Jehoshaphat, Jehoram, do with his brothers once his kingdom was established? _____

2. How did Joash forsake the LORD? _____

3. When Amaziah came home victorious by trusting God, how then did he forsake the LORD? _____

4. Uzziah did what was right in the eyes of the LORD, until his downfall. What was it? _____

5. How did Jotham grow so powerful? _____

6. How old was Hezekiah when he began to reign and what kind of man was he? _____

7. Sennacherib wrote and spoke against Hezekiah and the LORD, and intended to make war against Jerusalem. What happened to him? _____

8. How old was Josiah when he began to seek the LORD? _____

9. Who was king when Nebuchadnezzar, king of Babylon, first invaded Jerusalem? _____

10. How long was Israel held in captivity in Babylon before the decree by Cyrus, king of Persia, to let them go back home? _____

Week 19: Journey Through Ezra

The book begins with the 70 years of captivity ending, and with the first wave of the children of Israel returning to their homeland, Jerusalem. The king of Persia, who had defeated Babylon, decreed that the Jews could go home and rebuild their temple. He gave them all of the articles that belonged in the temple. They completed the work of rebuilding the temple.

Ezra, who was a scribe and a priest, led the second wave of people back to find that, yes, the temple was rebuilt, but the people had fallen into great sin. They had not been faithful, but had intermarried with the heathen nations and were serving other gods. Ezra was heartbroken, but prayed for them and led them to a national revival. He turned their hearts back to God.

Dear God, as we continue to read through Your Word, please help each one of us to see ourselves and to begin to change what needs to be changed in us. Help us to draw closer to You each and every day. We do love You the best! Please and thank You! In Jesus' name I pray. Amen!

Journey Through the Bible in Eleven Months

Questions Week 19 – Ezra Chapters 1-10

1. When did construction of the (new) house begin? _____
   _____

2. Who were the people appointed to supervise the building of the house of the LORD?
   _____
   _____

3. What was Ezra's job? _____
   _____
   _____

4. What did the people of Israel do that caused Ezra to sit down in astonishment? _____
   _____
   _____

Week 19: Journey Through Nehemiah

The book of Nehemiah goes with the book of Ezra. Nehemiah was very upset when he heard that the walls of Jerusalem had not been rebuilt. God placed His desire in Nehemiah's heart to go and rebuild the walls. As the cupbearer to the king, he was responsible for the wine, insuring there was no poison. When the king saw that Nehemiah was upset he gave him permission to go and rebuild the walls of Jerusalem.

Nehemiah was the leader of the third wave of God's people to go back to Jerusalem. He brought the people together and in 52 days the walls were rebuilt. Of course, any time we try to do God's work, there is going to be opposition. Nehemiah trusted God every step of the way and had success in the rebuilding of the walls. Once this was accomplished, Ezra stands to read the book of the law of Moses in the presence of the people. They listened to their history and learned where they had come from. As a result of hearing the law, they agreed to follow the Lord their God with all their hearts.

PEEK AT MY PRAYER

Dear God, You are holy and mighty, and You know each one of us. Help us, Lord, to follow closely after You. When we, like the children of Israel, sin against You, bring us back to a good relationship with You. Please and thank You! In Jesus' name I pray. Amen!

Journey Through the Bible in Eleven Months

Questions Week 19 – Nehemiah Chapters 1-13

1. What was Nehemiah's job for the king? _____

2. What was the desire of Nehemiah's heart? _____
   _____

3. Who opposed Nehemiah and what was the extent of this opposition? _____
   _____
   _____

4. What did Nehemiah ask the LORD for concerning all that he had done for the people?
   _____
   _____

5. How long did it take to rebuild the wall? _____

6. Why were the Ammonites and the Moabites banned from the Assembly of God forever?
   _____
   _____

7. Nehemiah reads like a diary. What was his last entry? _____
   _____
   _____

Week 20: Journey Through Esther

The book of Esther is the only book in the entire Bible that does not mention God by name, but it is very evident that He is the one in control.

Esther is a young Jewish girl, who is used by God to save the children of Israel. You will meet a man intent on destroying the Jews, because he thinks more highly of himself than he should. He is in a place of authority and realizes that he will not be honored by the Jews. He comes up with a plan to kill them. You will also meet a man who, when he learns about the plot, goes to Esther, who is the queen, and tells her that she must go to the king. She is hesitant at first, but tells him to have everybody to pray and fast for her. God is in control!

Dear God, thank You for showing us that even when we don't feel it, You are in control of our lives. You are excellent in all Your ways. Help us to continue on this journey through life knowing that You are with us. We do love you! Please and thank You! In Jesus' name I pray. Amen!

Journey Through the Bible in Eleven Months

Questions Week 20 – Esther Chapters 1-10

1. Why did King Ahasuerus decree that Queen Vashti come no more into his presence?

2. Who raised Esther, and what was her Jewish name?

3. Why do you think that Haman wanted to destroy the Jews?

4. When Esther was hesitant to go to the king, what did Mordecai say to her?

5. Haman hated Mordecai. How was he made to honor him?

6. What became of Haman and his 10 sons?

7. The Jews still celebrate their victory. What is this celebration called?

Weeks 20 – 21: Journey Through Job

In the life of Job, we see a man counted as righteous by God, and suffer unimaginable loss. The enemy of God tries to make Job turn his back on God. His friends, who sit with him, give many speeches and reasons for Job's suffering. Sin, they say, is the reason and they tell him to just admit it. Job maintains his innocence and just wants to plead his case before God. God will answer Job through a series of questions that truly leave him speechless and humbled. He learns that no matter what happens, God is with him.

Job is a man of integrity loved by God. His life teaches us that not all suffering is the result of sin. God sometimes just wants to bring us a little closer to Himself!

Father God, You are the light of our lives. You are the one that we trust the most. No matter what goes on in our lives God, we will trust You. Help us Lord to recognize You every step of the way on this journey. Bless those that have come this far. Please and thank You! In Jesus' name I pray. Amen!

Journey Through the Bible in Eleven Months

Questions Week 20 – Job Chapters 1-17

1. What kind of man was Job, and how many sons and daughters did he have? _____

2. Who came with the sons of God when they presented themselves before God?
   _____

3. What authority did God give to Satan concerning Job? _____

4. What did Job do and say when he heard that he had lost everything? _____
   _____
   _____
   _____

5. What did Job tell his wife when she told him to curse God and die? _____

6. How long did Job's friends sit with him before anyone spoke? _____

7. When Job first spoke, what did he say? _____

8. What did Bildad say about the death of Job's children? _____
   _____

9. Job's three friends keep telling him that he is guilty of sin. What are some of his responses? _____
   _____

10. What was Job's desire of God? _____

11. What are some of the things that Job says about his three friends? _____
    _____

Journey Through Job

Questions Week 21 – Job Chapters 18-42

1. Give one reason from each of Job's three friends as to why he was suffering and give a reply from him. _____

2. After more speeches from the three friends, what does Job say in his defense? _____

3. When God answers Job, where does He speak from? _____

4. When God asks a series of questions, how does Job answer? _____

5. What does Job say when he repents to God? _____

6. God was angry with Job's friends. What did He tell them to do? _____

7. What did everyone who had known Job do for him? _____

8. How did God bless Job in his latter years? _____

I ACCEPT

I accept the torment if it will make me stronger.

I accept the pain if it will make me grow.

I accept the unacceptable if it will make me understand.

I accept the test if it will make me pass.

I accept the loneliness if it will give me peace.

I accept the separation if it will bring me closer.

I accept the criticism if it will make me better.

I accept the trembling if it will make me be still.

I accept the cloudiness if it will make me to see clearly.

I accept the disappointments, the sadness, and the chaos
That life throws my way, but only if it will make me a better person.

Weeks 22 – 27: Journey Through Psalms

I was once told that the book of Psalms is the very heart of God. It teaches us that no matter what situation you may find yourself in, praise is always in order. I am reminded of a good hot shower, in that it relieves stress, it will wash away burdens, and it will refresh the soul. A few of the writers of Psalms include: David, the apple of God's eye; Solomon, the wisest man to ever live; and even Moses, the man that led God's people out of Egypt. Every Psalm is a song and as you read them, "listen" for the ones that we still sing today. There truly is strength and comfort in the pages of this book. I've often thought that it should be called heart to heart, from His heart to ours.

Dear God, help us to understand that even in our difficult times, You are still speaking to us through Your Holy Word. Teach us to always depend and trust in You, and You alone. We do love You so much. Please and thank You! In Jesus' name I do pray. Amen!

Journey Through the Bible in Eleven Months

Questions Week 22 – Psalms Numbers 1-25

1. What is the delight of a blessed man? (Psalm 1) _____

2. Who has God set apart for Himself? (Psalm 4) _____

3. What does the psalmist say about the morning? (Psalm 5) _____

4. Why does the psalmist tell the workers of iniquity to depart from him? (Psalm 6) _____

5. What does David say is his defense? (Psalm 7) _____

6. Whom has the LORD never forsaken? (Psalm 9) _____

7. The LORD examines/tries the righteous. What will He do for the wicked? (Psalm 11) _____

8. What does a fool say in his heart? (Psalm 14) _____

9. How does God show Himself to the merciful, the upright, and the pure? (Psalm 18) _____

10. Who shall ascend the hill of the LORD? (Psalm 24) _____

Journey Through Psalms

Questions Week 23 – Psalms Numbers 26-50

1. What is the one thing that David desires and will seek of the LORD? (Psalm 27)

2. How long does God's anger last; how long His favor? (Psalm 30)

3. What has God stored up for those who fear Him? (Psalm 31)

4. What does the LORD give to those that delight themselves in Him? (Psalm 37)

5. What is the thirst and the joy of David in Psalm 42?

6. God tells the songwriter to be still. Why? (Psalm 46)

7. How do these first 50 psalms speak to you? Remember that psalms are songs.

Journey Through the Bible in Eleven Months

Questions Week 24 – Psalms Numbers 51-75

1. David pleads from his heart for forgiveness. What had he done? (Psalm 51) _____

2. Again, what does the fool say? (Psalm 53) _____

3. Where does God's mercy and truth reach to? (Psalm 57) _____

4. Where does David ask God to lead him when his heart is overwhelmed? (Psalm 61)

5. What does the writer say will worship God? (Psalm 66) _____

6. How long does David say that he has trusted in God? (Psalm 71) _____

7. What does the LORD pour out that all the wicked of the earth shall drink? (Psalm 75)

Journey Through Psalms

Questions Week 25 – Psalms Numbers 76-100

1. Psalm 77 mentions the thunder, the lightnings, and the earth. What is said about each?

2. Psalm 78 is a story. What is the story? Who does it begin with, and who does it end with?

3. What does God do for those whose trust is in Him and walk upright? (Psalm 84)

4. Psalm 91 is a beautiful picture of God's love. Please, in your own words, describe how it touches you.

5. Psalm 94 speaks of the proud, the wicked, and the evil doers. What is their end?

6. How should the people of God serve Him, and why? (Psalm 100)

Journey Through the Bible in Eleven Months

Questions Week 26 – Psalms Numbers 101-125

1. What is said about the faithful and what is said about the wicked? (Psalm 101) _____

2. Psalm 103 praises God. In your own words, name some of the good things about Him.

3. Psalm 105 is a snapshot of a part of Israel's history. Name the people it talks about and what you know about each of them.

4. What is the beginning of wisdom? (Psalm 111) _____

5. Which psalm is the shortest, with how many verses? _____

6. Which psalm is the longest, with how many verses? _____

7. Who does the psalmist ask God to be good to? (Psalm 125) _____

Journey Through Psalms

Questions Week 27 – Psalms Numbers 126-150

1. When the LORD brought the captives back to Zion, how do they describe themselves? (Psalm 126) _____
   _____
   _____

2. The LORD swore a truth to David. What was that truth, and what were the conditions of it? (Psalm 132) _____
   _____
   _____

3. Describe the idols of the heathen. (Psalm 135) _____
   _____
   _____

4. What is the theme of Psalm 136? _____
   _____
   _____
   _____

5. For how long and when does the psalmist say that he will praise the name of God? (Psalm 145) _____
   _____
   _____

6. What do the last five Psalms have in common? How do they start, and how do they end?
   _____
   _____
   _____

   Extra Credit: What is the oldest Psalm and who wrote it? _____
   _____

Journey Through the Bible in Eleven Months

Week 28: Journey Through Proverbs

So, if Psalms is the heart of God, then surely the Proverbs are His mind. The wisdom and guidance contained in the pages of this book can always bring tears to my eyes. It helps us to live in a world that is contrary to what the Lord expects from us. Solomon is the writer of most of this book and God used him mightily. He let God pour into him, and then was able to write down these proverbs.

Since Psalms is a good hot shower, let's see the Proverbs as a good hot bath. We will submerge ourselves to get wisdom, we will soak up the knowledge, and we will linger to get the understanding that our God intends for us. As we read and think about these sayings, we should let them get down into the very core of our hearts!

PEEK AT MY PRAYER

Good Morning Father, thank You so much for Your love and care towards us. You are beyond compare and You are wonderful. Keep us in Your precious Word and help us to understand what You are saying to each one of us. We do love You! Please and thank You! In Jesus' name I pray. Amen!

Journey Through Proverbs

Questions Week 28 – Proverbs Chapters 1-31

1. Who wrote most of the book of Proverbs? What is a proverb for? _____

2. How are we to seek and search for understanding? _____

3. Why should we not despise the LORD's chastening and his correction? _____

4. What is the way of the wicked? _____

5. What does Solomon say about the strange woman and what is her end? _____

6. When was wisdom brought forth? _____

7. What do the Proverbs say about he who spares the rod? _____

8. What is the name of the LORD? _____

9. What does the candle of the LORD do? _____

10. Who will have the king for his friend? _____

11. What should we do for our enemy and why? _____

12. Who is Proverbs 31 associated with? _____

Journey Through the Bible in Eleven Months

YOU ARE MY FATHER

You are my A B C's Lord, and my 1 2 3's.
You are my basic and my complex in all that I do.
Can I tell you some words of how I feel about you?

1. *You are my agent, my always, my air, Abba.*
2. *You are my bridegroom, my biggest, and my best brother.*
3. *You are my confidant, my constant, my caress.*
4. *You are my defender, my direction, my deep, Daddy.*
5. *You are my energy, my excitement, and my every day.*
6. *You are my first, my friend, my forever, Father.*
7. *You are my good, my great, my go, and my God.*
8. *You are my heart, my humble, and my help.*
9. *You are my indeed, my instant, my innocence.*
10. *You are my joy, my jolly, my justified Jesus.*
11. *You are my knight, my kisses, my kind King.*
12. *You are my lover, my large, and my Lord.*
13. *You are my magic, my martyr, and my most.*
14. *You are my nearest, my naked, my now.*
15. *You are my one, my open, my overcomer.*
16. *You are my past, my present, my pure Papa.*
17. *You are my quick, my quaint, and my quiet.*
18. *You are my rock, my real, my Rah.*
19. *You are my steady, my safety, and my sure.*
20. *You are my teacher, my truth, and my tears.*
21. *You are my under, my undisputed, my umbrella.*
22. *You are my vast, my valley, and my victor.*
23. *You are my wide, my world, my will, and my witness.*
24. *You are my x-ray, my xenial, and my xerography.*
25. *You are my youth, my years, my yearning.*
26. *You are my zest, my zenith, my zeal.*

You are my A B C's Lord, and my 1 2 3's.
You are my basic and my complex in all that I do.
Can I tell you some words of how I feel about you?

Week 29: Journey Through Ecclesiastes

In this book, the writer tells us that there is nothing new under the sun, that there is a time for everything, and that some things in life are like chasing the wind. He sets out to see if life in this world without God has any worth (hint: hint: it most certainly does not!).

You see, when we leave God out, we will always be found lacking and void. When we fill our lives with God, we are enriched far beyond anything that the world can offer. Anything apart from Him is vanity; the teacher/preacher does let us know that apart from God, life is meaningless.

Good Morning Father, today I do pray for everyone that may be doing this study, bless us with Your wisdom that You so freely give. Thank You again for Your beautiful Word! Please and thank You! In Jesus' name I pray. Amen!

Journey Through the Bible in Eleven Months

Questions Week 29 – Ecclesiastes Chapters 1-12

1. Who wrote the book of Ecclesiastes? _____

2. What comes with much wisdom and more knowledge? _____

3. The wise man has eyes in his head, and the fool walks in darkness; what fate overtakes them both? _____

4. To what is there a season and a time? _____

5. What did the writer see in the place of judgment and in the place of righteousness? _____

6. How serious is a vow to God? _____

7. What is said about a good name and about the day of death? _____

8. What is the conclusion of the whole matter in the book of Ecclesiastes? _____

Week 29: Journey Through Song of Solomon

On the surface, this book seems to be about the love between a man and a woman. It is so much more! Moreover, on another level, it is about the love that God has for His people, again it is so much more. I say this because of a study that I participated in, in which the teacher broke it down verse by verse. This study lasted just about two years and every part of it was good. It was an amazing study in which we learned that God loves us so much, that He patiently romances us into a deeper, higher, wider, and an all-encompassing intimate relationship with Him. Listen as He calls us beautiful and watch as He puts us in royal clothing. His love for us is truly overwhelming!

Good Morning Lord, today we ask that You help us to keep our focus on the things above. As we study, open our hearts and minds. Please and thank You! In Jesus' name I pray. Amen!

Journey Through the Bible in Eleven Months

Questions Week 29 – Song of Solomon Chapters 1-8

1. How does the Shulammite woman describe herself?

2. What does her beloved say to her when the winter is past?

3. What has the man's wife ravished/stolen from him, and how did she do it?

4. Where does the wife ask her husband to set her?

Chapter Six – The Bad Day

FRIDAY . . . She loved Fridays, the last day of the week. When she woke up that Friday morning, she had a feeling of unease. She felt in her spirit that something just wasn't right. There was almost a sense of confusion, but not really.

The mornings were her favorite part of the day. She got up early and had the house to herself to do her normal. She would go to the kitchen, put the coffee on, go to her praying place to spend time with the Lord, and then sit at her desk. She was working on a book and was very excited about it. She felt that the Lord had assigned her to do it. She loved the mornings, especially Friday mornings.

The book or the program was an instrument that she hoped and prayed God would make available to those with a hunger for Him. It was designed to take people through the Bible in 11 months, and she believed with all her heart that God was guiding and orchestrating it. She was amazed that He would use her to do such a thing, and she was excited and humbled. It was designed to take the reader from Genesis to Revelation. She made a reading schedule. She had an introduction to each book. Also, there were questions and answers to test the knowledge of what had been read within the week. She just happened to be working on the book of Isaiah that Friday morning when everything seemed to be off kilter.

Journey Through the Bible in Eleven Months

Weeks 30 – 31: Journey Through Isaiah

Isaiah is considered one of the major prophets because of the length of his prophecy. He covers the time of four kings and writes extensively about the coming Messiah. God used Isaiah to deliver a message for the time in which he lived. This same message is relative to the time in which we live. He lets the people know that judgment is coming because of their sin of forsaking God, turning to other gods and blatant disobedience. He tells them that they will go into captivity, but because of the love that God has for them, they will come out of their bondage.

Isaiah has 66 chapters and within these pages, he also prophesied about the Messiah, the Lord Jesus. He tells of the sign of His lowly birth, His terrible death, and everything that He would do to redeem His people. He sees into the future to a new heaven and a new earth, when Jesus will come back as the Almighty King, to rule and to reign.

PEEK AT MY PRAYER

Good Morning Father, as we journey through Your Word, help us to not give up and to stay on this course. Help us to understand what it is that You want "me" to get from Your Word. Please and thank You! In Jesus' name I pray. Amen!

Journey Through Isaiah

Questions Week 30 – Isaiah Chapters 1-33

1. What does God say about the offerings, the incense, the new moons, and the festivals that the people brought? _____

2. What does God have in store for all the proud and lofty and all that is lifted up? _____

3. What is the vineyard of the LORD? What did He see and hear there? _____

4. How does Isaiah respond when God asks, "Whom shall I send?" and "Who will go for us?" _____

5. The people have wearied God, and because of this, what sign does He give them? _____

6. What is said concerning the people walking in darkness and those living in the shadow of death? _____

7. Where do we find the prophecy that calls Jesus Wonderful, Counselor, Mighty God, Everlasting Father, and Prince of Peace? _____

8. Who is the root of Jesse and what will he do in the day of the LORD? _____

9. What is the theme for chapters 13-23? _____

10. Who is the son of the morning? What does he say that he will do, and what is his end? _____

11. What is the work and effect of righteousness? _____

Journey Through the Bible in Eleven Months

Questions Week 31 – Isaiah Chapters 34-66

1. What was Isaiah told to say to those with fearful hearts? _____
_____
_____

2. In what year of Hezekiah's reign did Assyria attack and capture Judah? _____
_____

3. How many Assyrians did the angel of the LORD smote/kill in their camp? _____

4. What did Hezekiah do that was not very wise? _____
_____

5. What were the consequences of his actions? _____
_____

6. What does Isaiah say about those that wait/hope in the LORD? _____
_____
_____

7. What does God say to His people about the waters, the rivers, and the fire? _____
_____
_____
_____
_____

8. Who is Chapter 53 about, and what does it say about His appearance? _____
_____
_____
_____

9. Who was God found by that was not seeking for Him? _____
_____

Extra Credit: Is Isaiah a major or minor prophet? ❑ Major ❑ Minor Why? _____
_____
_____

Chapter Seven – The Bad Got Worse

As she typed out what had already been handwritten, the unease that hovered over her seemed to thicken. "What is it, Lord?" But she kept on typing: the Journey Through Isaiah; the prayer for Isaiah; and the questions and answers for Isaiah. She wanted to get this finished before going to work. A small sigh of relief escaped her as she finished and hit the print key. She went to the printer to gather all of the pages together to put in a folder marked, "Master." When she opened the folder, she stopped right in her tracks. There lying on top, was the copy of Isaiah. She had two copies of the same book. She just stood there dumbfounded. "Oh God," she whispered. "What's going on? How did I do this book twice?" From that point on, she knew to her very core that something was wrong and didn't know what it was.

In a daze, she went to work and just went through the motions. She felt detached from herself and thought that maybe she was losing her mind. She sounded out three different people, and told them what had happened, and did her best to make them understand that this was not like her, not like her at all. Each of these three confidants said the same thing, "It seems as though the Lord wants to show you something in the book of Isaiah." She just wasn't convinced, just felt like she was losing her mind.

Her work for the day was light and she was able to get off early. She went straight home, which was not like her at all. As she pulled into the driveway, she saw that her grass had not been cut. Her husband had assured her that he would cut it. She hated tall grass; maybe he was having a bad day, too.

Still trying to wrap her mind around the events of that morning, she went straight to her room, took off her shoes, and got into the bed. The clock read one o'clock. "Oh Father, please help me," she said as she pulled the covers up over herself. She thought that maybe a nap would make her feel better, and she felt herself be pulled into sleep. When she opened her eyes, the clock read five o'clock, and she didn't feel any better. The depression made her want to turn over and go back to sleep. She pulled herself up out of the bed and thought that maybe a hot bath would help her to feel better. She ran the water as hot as she could bear and eased her depressed body into it. She heard her husband when he came in, but she didn't call out to him, and he didn't call out to her. She stayed in the tub until the water was no longer hot. She wanted to let it out and start all over again with hot water. She didn't feel better, only cleaner.

Her husband was at the table eating when she came out. One look at her and he knew that something was wrong. "What's wrong with you?" he asked. "Nothing." She said, "Nothing." She wanted so badly to tell him about her terrible day; wanted to tell him that she felt that she was losing her mind. She desperately wanted to tell him that from the time she had gotten up, everything was off. If only she could make him understand about the anxiety, the foreboding, and the depression that had commanded her attention all day long up to this very moment, maybe she would feel better. But she didn't, and he did not ask again. It was like him to not probe; maybe he was having a bad day, too.

Weeks 32 – 33: Journey Through Jeremiah

Jeremiah is another major prophet called by God at a very young age. He does not really want to go and "tell the people" anything, but he is very faithful to the Lord. He is told that the people would not listen to him, but that he must go and tell them of the coming doom and destruction. The people are in a decline when it comes to God. They are rebelling against the God who has loved them unconditionally. They have left off following Him and have disregarded His laws. Jeremiah does deliver the message that they will go into captivity, and that they will be slaves to foreigners in a strange land. But, because of the great love that God has for them, they will be set free to return to the homeland.

Jeremiah was not believed. He was beaten, he was thrown into prison, and still he did what God told him to do. He had compassion for the people and would often intercede on their behalf, but the Lord told him, "Do not pray for the well-being of this people." He is often referred to as the weeping prophet.

Good Morning Father, thank You for the honor of getting to know You through Your Word. Help us to meditate on the things that we learn and apply them to our own lives. Please and thank You! In Jesus' name we pray. Amen!

Journey Through the Bible in Eleven Months

Questions Week 32 – Jeremiah Chapters 1-31

1. Who was the king when the word of the LORD came to Jeremiah and what did God say to him? _____

2. When the LORD says to Judah and Jerusalem to circumcise yourselves to the LORD, what will happen if they didn't? _____

3. God tells Jeremiah to go up and down the streets of Jerusalem and find someone. Who was he trying to find? What would God do if he found them? _____

4. God says that a wonderful and horrible thing has happened in the land. What was it? _____

5. What does God say about the people, from the least to the greatest, and from the prophets to the priests? _____

6. In Chapter 7, what commandments were being broken? _____

7. What does the LORD say about the wise man, the mighty man, and the rich man? _____

8. What did God tell Jeremiah that he must not do concerning a wife and children? _____

9. What does God say about the prophet and the priest? _____

Journey Through Jeremiah

10. Who was the king of Babylon at the time that the nation of Israel was taken into captivity?
    _____

11. What did Jeremiah tell the whole land about their captivity and how long it would last?
    _____
    _____

12. What happened to the false prophets Ahab and Zedekiah? _____
    _____

Questions Week 33 – Jeremiah Chapters 32-52

1. What did the king do with the scroll dictated by Jeremiah to Baruch, to be read to the people? _____
    _____
    _____

2. What happened to Zedekiah, king of Judah, after the fall of Jerusalem? _____
    _____
    _____

3. The remnant asked Jeremiah to pray on their behalf. What did they want to know?
    _____
    _____

4. Jeremiah warned the remnant not to go to Egypt. Why? _____
    _____

5. What did God say Nebuchadnezzar would do to the land of Egypt? _____
    _____

6. What does God say about Edom in relation to Sodom and Gomorrah? _____
    _____

7. How many Jews were taken captive by Nebuchadnezzar? _____

Chapter Eight – Could It Get Any Worse?

Saturday . . . When she opened her eyes, she felt better, a whole lot better. Yesterday was gone, and today was a brand-new day. "Thank You, Lord," she whispered. "Today I'm not gonna work on the program, maybe I just need a break."

She usually worked on the program every day. It was a labor of love, and it excited her every morning when she could sit at her desk for a while and get lost in the Word of God. She had been working on it for about six months straight and was about halfway through when she hit the snag yesterday.

She got up, feeling relieved that she did feel better. As she went towards the bathroom, she saw that the light was on in the room where her husband slept. "He didn't take a shower?" she thought. He always took a shower. If he fell asleep, when he woke up, he always took a shower. He was lying across the bed with his clothes on, and he still had his shoes on. "Man," she thought, "He was really tired." She called his name, but he didn't move. She called louder. As she stepped up to the bed, he didn't move. She reached out and shook his foot, panic rising as he didn't move. Now she was screaming his name and telling him to wake up. She ran around to the other side of the bed and started shaking him and screaming his name. Tears were rolling down her face as she shook him harder and willed him to wake up. "Wake up!" she yelled. "Wake up!" She ran to the kitchen and dialed 911. "I can't wake my husband up, please help me. I can't wake my husband up, oh God, oh dear God, I can't wake my husband up."

So many families and friends came and for the rest of the day, she was in a daze. She couldn't tell you anything about anything. Her heart was shattered. She almost felt as though he had just left her. She could not comprehend everything that was going on. She knew that she had talked to her dad and her kids. She knew that they would be there as soon as they could. She had spoken to so many people. But mainly she spoke to the LORD. She was so aware of His presence that she knew that it was Him that was leading her through. After everyone left and the house was quiet, she took her Bible to the kitchen table, sat down, and just opened it. It opened to the book of ISAIAH. As she stared at it, the tears started flowing until they were a flood, and she couldn't have stopped them. She cried like she had never cried before, and she could not tell you what was written on the page. Through the pain and the tears, she bowed her head and said, "Thank You Father!"

Week 33: Journey Through Lamentations

The book of Lamentations is believed to have been written by the prophet Jeremiah. He is lamenting, or crying out loud, over the doom and destruction of Jerusalem. He cries because the people are not listening to the warnings of God. We hear depression and despair coming from this great man of God. As he looks upon the downfall of his once great nation, he is full of anguish, and his very heart is broken. But within his shattered heart, he has hope, hope for his people because he knows of the great love that God has for them. He knows that no matter how bleak or dire situations are, we must always have hope in our Lord, who is able to change all things.

Good Morning Father, today help each one of us to lean on the hope that is in You. Walk with us on this journey that is not always easy. Please and thank You! In Jesus' name I pray. Amen!

Journey Through the Bible in Eleven Months

Questions Week 33 – Lamentations Chapters 1-5

1. How does the writer describe the deserted city once so full? _____
   _____
   _____

2. Because there is no comfort for him, what does the writer do? _____
   _____
   _____

3. Why is the nation not completely destroyed or consumed? _____
   _____
   _____

   Extra Credit 1: What does the word Lamentations mean? _____
   _____

   Extra Credit 2: Who is the writer of this book and what is his nickname? _____
   _____

   Extra Credit 3: Sum up the book of Lamentations in your own words. _____
   _____
   _____
   _____

Weeks 34 – 35: Journey Through Ezekiel

Ezekiel was another major prophet who came from a family of priests. He prophesied of the coming judgment, he was taken into captivity by Nebuchadnezzar, and he told the people of a future full of blessings.

He was shown visions by God and was also spoken to in parables. Ezekiel kept reminding the people of the reason they were in captivity; because of sin. He also let them know that God had not forsaken them, and that there was a future of blessings.

God will allow us to go into "captivity," but because of his great love for us, there is always a place of restoration.

Precious Lord, thank You so much for never leaving us or forsaking us. You are good and You are gentle with us. Please help us as we continue on this journey called life. Please and thank You! In Jesus' name I pray. Amen!

Journey Through the Bible in Eleven Months

Questions Week 34 – Ezekiel Chapters 1-30

1. What was Ezekiel's job? _____

2. When God first speaks to Ezekiel, how does He address him? _____

3. God told Ezekiel to lie on his left side for a certain number of days for the sin of Israel and to lie on his right side a certain number of days for the sin of Judah. How many days for each side and what did the days represent? _____

4. In one vision, God tells a man clothed in linen with a writer's inkhorn to go throughout the city and do what? _____

5. In the vision of the cherubim, each one had four faces. What were they? _____

6. When a righteous man turns from his righteousness and commits sin, and does the same abominable things the wicked man does, what becomes of all the good he has done? _____

7. What happens to a wicked man who turns from his wickedness? _____

8. What metals does the LORD say that the house of Israel has become? _____

9. Where will the LORD put the house of Israel in His anger (the different metals)? _____

10. What year, month, and day did the king of Babylon set himself against Jerusalem? _____

11. What did the LORD take from Ezekiel, which was the desire of his eyes, and forbid him to do when it happened? _____

12. Who, besides the king of Tyre, could the LORD be speaking to in Chapter 28? Give some verses of proof. _____
_____
_____

Questions Week 35 – Ezekiel Chapters 31-48

1. When the trumpet sounded, what happened to those who took the warning and those that did not? _____
_____
_____

2. When the spirit of the LORD carried Ezekiel out and set him down in the valley, what was the valley full of? _____
_____

3. From which gate did Ezekiel see the glory of the LORD come? _____
_____

4. On what day and month was the house of Israel to observe the Passover, and how long was it to last? _____
_____

I SAY ~ YOU SAY

I say: Lord, sometimes I feel so all alone.
You say: Child **I Am** with you always!

I say: Oh Father, I seem to cry all the time.
You say: Little one, your tears are precious to me.

I say: God, I don't know about tomorrow.
You say: Love, **I Am** your past, your present, and your future.

I say: Sir, how can You love me so much?
You say: Because you are my child.

I say: Holy One, sometimes I am afraid.
You say: I have not given you a spirit of fear!

I say: Eternal One, sometimes this life just isn't fair.
You say: I will take care of that!

I say: Ancient of days, why me?
You say: Because when I called, you came!

I say: And what about the stormy times when the thunder is cracking and the lightning is flashing, and the rain is coming down so hard that I feel like I'm drowning? What then my protector?
You say: Child, my precious little child, just be still and know that **I Am** God.

Week 35: Journey Through Daniel

Daniel is the fourth and final major prophet. As a youngster, he was taken into Babylonian captivity and spent the rest of his life there. He was a prophet who also just happened to work for the government (God will place us in strategic places). Even though he worked for a heathen nation, he was very faithful to God and was used mightily by Him. Daniel was also an interpreter of dreams, a gift that was given to him by God. He has three friends who, because of their faith, are thrown into a hot, hot, hot fiery furnace. You will witness a scheme against Daniel that lands him in a den of lions, but God's glory is shown, when he comes out unharmed. God will show Daniel visions of the future that frighten him. Daniel will converse with angels sent to minster to him. As you read the story of his life, you will see our God lead and guide him through every step.

Good Morning Father, thank You so much for the example of faith lived out in the life of Daniel. Help our faith to be just like his. We do trust You with this journey through life. We want to please You in everything that we do, so Father, walk us through every moment. Please and thank You! In Jesus' name I pray. Amen!

Journey Through the Bible in Eleven Months

Questions Week 35 – Daniel Chapters 1-12

1. What were the names given by the chief official to Daniel and his three friends? _____

2. What special gift given by God did Daniel and his friends have? _____

3. What did Nebuchadnezzar shout when he saw four men in the fiery furnace? _____

4. Who represents the large, strong tree that reaches into heaven? _____

5. What made King Belshazzar so afraid that his knees knocked? _____

6. How was Daniel saved from the lions? _____

7. What is happening when we see the Ancient of days? _____

8. Daniel was told by a man dressed in linen, that from the start of his prayer, his words were heard. Why did it take three weeks for a response to reach him? _____

Week 36: Journey Through Hosea

The prophet Hosea was told by God to go and marry a woman who was adulterous and unfaithful to him. His love for her was so great, that even when she left him to follow after and to be with other men, he would go and get her. He even had to pay a price to redeem her back to himself. His love for her was so great.

This unfaithful wife represents the children of Israel, and Hosea represents the loving God who would always redeem His children back to Himself. The God of our lives loves us unconditionally. We stumble, we fall, and sometimes we stray so far from Him that only His great love can bring us back. He is so good!

Good Morning Father, thank You for a love that is pure, and unconditional. Help us dear Lord to never take that love for granted, but to always be grateful and thankful to You. Please and thank You! In Jesus' name I pray. Amen!

Journey Through the Bible in Eleven Months

Questions Week 36 – Hosea Chapters 1-14

1. What was the name of Hosea's adulterous wife? _____

2. What did Hosea pay for the adulterous woman, and what did he say to her? _____
   _____
   _____
   _____

3. What was the controversy that God had against those that lived in the land? _____
   _____
   _____

4. What kind of a spirit does God say is in the midst of the people that they will not turn unto Him? _____

5. What does God desire more than sacrifice and more than burnt offerings? _____
   _____

6. Because of their wickedness in Gilgal, what does God say about the children of Israel?
   _____
   _____

7. How does God bless Israel when they return to Him? _____
   _____
   _____

Week 36: Journey Through Joel

The prophet Joel sees the invasion to his homeland, by the enemy, like swarms of locusts. They come in waves to conquer, to destroy, and to devour until there is nothing left. He will tell the children of Israel that "the day of the Lord" is close, that their sin is great, and that God is angry with them. Decisions need to be made and he wants them to know that all they have to do is return to the Lord with their whole hearts. If they do, then God is faithful to bless them tremendously. Sincerely give your heart to the Father!

Dear God, please forgive us. We are sorry for the times when we are wayward, and when we go in the wrong direction. We will always need Your loving kindness in our everyday lives. Help us dear Lord to be led by You. Please and thank You! In Jesus' name I pray. Amen!

Questions Week 36 – Joel Chapters 1-3

1. Name the insect(s) that have devoured the land. _____
   _____

2. Why does Joel tell the drunkards to weep and to wail? _____
   _____
   _____

3. When God says that He will pour out His spirit on all people, what will those people do? _____
   _____

4. What happens and who will God save and deliver from the great and terrible day of the LORD? _____

5. What will God do in the valley of Jehoshaphat? _____
   _____
   _____
   _____

Journey Through Amos

Week 36: Journey Through Amos

Amos was a shepherd who was used by God to pronounce judgment on many heathen nations, as well as on the children of Israel. God's people had gone astray. They, like the heathen nations, were following other gods. They rejected the law of the true and living God. They used their wealth to treat those who were less fortunate very badly.

God did everything to cause them to return to Him, but they were a stiff-necked people and would not listen to Him. Because they were loved and chosen by God, their doom was great.

Dear God, help us, Your chosen people, to not go after anything that is not in Your will for us. You are our leader and our guide. Please and thank You! In Jesus' name I pray. Amen!

✝✝

Questions Week 36 – Amos Chapters 1-9

1. What was the occupation of Amos? _____

2. When evil is in a city, what is the cause? _____
   _____

3. Amos tells the house of Israel that they shall seek the LORD. Why? _____
   _____

4. What does Amos say that the day of the LORD will be? _____
   _____

5. What kind of famine will the LORD send on the land? _____
   _____

Week 37: Journey Through Obadiah

While there is not much that is known about Obadiah, we do know that his name means "servant of God." His prophesy was aimed directly at Edom. Edomites were the descendants of Esau, the twin brother of Jacob (Israel). Just as there was a struggle while these two brothers were in the womb, there was also opposition throughout the generations. The Edomites were an arrogant people that not only came against the children of Israel, but were happy to see trouble come to them from others. Obadiah is a little short book, which spells doom for Edom.

Dear God, please help each one of us to be kind and loving towards our brothers and sisters. Teach us to pray for one another, and not bring each other down. Just help us to get along. Please and thank You! In Jesus' name we pray. Amen!

✝✝✝✝✝✝✝✝✝✝✝✝✝✝✝✝✝✝✝✝✝✝✝✝✝✝✝✝✝✝✝✝✝✝✝✝✝✝✝

Questions Week 37 – Obadiah Chapter 1

1. Why is this prophecy of Obadiah against Edom? Give four verses. _____
_____
_____
_____
_____
_____

Week 37: Journey Through Jonah

Jonah was a prophet sent to preach to a Gentile nation. He did not want to go and tried his hardest to get out of his assignment from God. He ran, got on a ship headed out to sea, was thrown overboard, got swallowed by a big fish, was thrown up out of the big fish, and ended up right back where he started from. (We just cannot run from God!) He went and preached to the Ninevites, and he must have preached real good, because they did repent. He became angry with God because of His mercy on this nation of people who were enemies of the children of Israel. God explained to Jonah that He loves everybody!

Good Morning Jesus, help us please to take every opportunity to be a light to a dark world. You work through each one of us. When You send us, we will go. Please and thank You! In your name we pray. Amen!

Journey Through the Bible in Eleven Months

Questions Week 37 – Jonah Chapters 1-4

1. What city was Jonah sent to prophesy against? Why? _____

2. Why did the sailors throw Jonah off of the ship in the middle of a great storm?

3. Why didn't Jonah drown? _____

4. What did the people do after hearing Jonah preach? _____

5. What was it that made Jonah so angry? _____

Week 37: Journey Through Micah

Micah was a prophet that had a message for the people of God. He proclaims to the people that because of their sin and their transgressions, judgment is coming and that God Himself, who is the witness against them, will also be their judge. Micah also has a message of judgment for the priests, the leaders, and the false prophets, because of their mistreatment of the common people. God gives him a glimpse into the future of the coming king and kingdom. He paints a picture of hope and security, if only the people would listen. God uses Micah to tell these people what is required of them and that in every situation they should trust Him.

Thank You dear Lord for the many, many blessings You have given to us. Help us to appreciate all that You do for us and never to take advantage of others. We love You. Please and thank You! In Jesus' name we pray. Amen!

Journey Through the Bible in Eleven Months

Questions Week 37 – Micah Chapters 1-7

1. Describe the way the earth responds when the LORD leaves His dwelling place to come down. _____

2. What were the leaders, the priests, and the prophets doing that should not have been done? _____

3. Where does the ruler, whose origins are from old and everlasting times, come from? _____

4. What did the LORD show the people that was good and what does He require of them? _____

5. Why does the prophet say that a man's enemies are the members of his own household? _____

Journey Through Nahum

Week 37: Journey Through Nahum

Our God! He had given a heathen nation a chance to repent and they did, but that was over 100 years ago (remember Nineveh). They have returned to their evil ways and now destruction will be their destination. Jonah preached repentance, and now Nahum, the prophet, is preaching the consequences of their sin. They are to be destroyed.

Hello Father, please help us always to remember Your forgiveness in our lives. Keep us each and every day Lord, and keep us on the path that leads to You. Please and thank You! In Jesus' name we pray. Amen!

✝✝✝

Questions Week 37 – Nahum Chapters 1-3

1. What city did Nahum prophesy against? _____

2. What does the prophet say about those that trust in the LORD and those that are His enemies? _____

3. What is said to the king about his shepherds, his nobles, and his people? What can heal them? _____

Week 37: Journey Through Habakkuk

The prophet Habakkuk was sent to the children of Israel just before they were invaded and taken into captivity by the Babylonians. He asks God some questions, because he wanted to understand why God would let His people get away with doing wrong, and why He would use the Babylonians (who were much worse) to punish His people. God does answer him, and he is content with the answers. His faith in God was great and he accepted the way that God did everything. He praised God in all things.

Dear God, sometimes we don't understand all that You do or why, but show us how to put our hope and trust in You at all times. Please and thank You! In Jesus' name we pray. Amen!

Journey Through Habakkuk

Questions Week 37 – Habakkuk Chapters 1-3

1. What are the first questions that Habakkuk asks God and why?

2. Habakkuk will stand watch until God tells him to write down the vision. What is the vision waiting for?

3. What happened physically to Habakkuk when he heard God moving through the land?

Journey Through the Bible in Eleven Months

Week 37: Journey Through Zephaniah

The prophet Zephaniah was born into royalty and was tasked with preaching a revival to the people of God. They heard him, and for a time they repented. But they soon returned to their wicked and evil ways. Zephaniah informs them that judgment is coming. He encourages them to seek the Lord. He also looks to the future and the coming of "the day of the Lord," where the enemies of God will be destroyed and the people of God will be welcomed into the kingdom.

Hello Father, let us always be mindful that You are in control and that if we stick with You, we can't lose. Forgive us when we mess up. Please and thank You! In Jesus name we pray. Amen!

Questions Week 37 – Zephaniah Chapters 1-3

1. Who was Zephaniah's great, great grandfather? _____

2. How does the prophet describe the day of the LORD? _____
   _____
   _____

3. What does Zephaniah say to the meek of the earth and why does he say it? _____
   _____
   _____

4. How does the LORD describe the leaders/officials in Jerusalem? _____
   _____
   _____

Week 37: Journey Through Haggai

Haggai was the voice that the people of God heard when they came out of the Babylonian captivity. He encouraged them to build the temple. They knew this was what the Lord wanted them to do, but they were procrastinating. Haggai told them that if they would complete the task, that the Lord would bless them.

Good Morning Father, we do ask that You help us with doing the things that You have assigned to us. Give us an enthusiastic heart for You! Please and thank You! In Jesus' name we pray. Amen!

✝✝

Questions Week 37 – Haggai Chapters 1-2

1. Why does God send Haggai to speak to the people? _____
   _____
   _____

2. What does God say about the present house of the LORD? _____
   _____
   _____
   _____

Journey Through the Bible in Eleven Months

YOU ARE ALWAYS NEAR

I remember Father when I first met You,
Your love is so pure, and Your love is so true.

You opened my eyes to the good and the bad;
You made me so happy when truly I was sad.

I see on my life You have placed a call;
You even catch me long before I fall.

You took the despair, and You took the fear.
You've made me understand that You are always near.

I need You to know that I love You so much;
I eagerly await Your most holy touch.

My feelings for You I cannot hide;
You sent the Lord Jesus and for me He died.

Please walk me through this life day by day,
And when I need to speak Lord, tell me what to say.

I realize Father that You made me stronger than I know.
And I will use that strength and continue to grow.

And when life becomes more than I can bear;
I'll run to Your throne room; I'll meet You there.

My feelings for You, God, I cannot mask;
Just don't let me go, that's all that I ask.

Week 38: Journey Through Zechariah

Zechariah was the prophet that called the people to repentance and encouraged them to finish the temple. Then he gives them hope for the future, if only they would obey. He comforts them with his visions of the future. He declares the blessings that God has for them. He predicts the first coming of the Messiah and sees into the far future to the Lord's second coming when He will rule and reign. We can take hope from the prophecy of Zechariah.

Thank You, Father, for the many blessings that You have freely given us. Forgive us Lord when we go astray and help us to always strive to be better. Please and thank You! In Jesus' name I pray. Amen!

Journey Through the Bible in Eleven Months

Questions Week 38 – Zechariah Chapters 1-14

1. Explain what the different colored horses go out and do. _____
_____
_____

2. What did the angel of the LORD protest unto Joshua, the high priest, once his raiment had been changed? _____
_____

3. What is said about the woman in the midst of an ephah? _____
_____

4. What do the chariots represent and where are they going? _____
_____

5. How does (Jesus) the gentle king, come to Zion and Jerusalem? _____
_____

6. The LORD says that two-thirds of all the land (people) shall be cut off and die. What will happen to the third that is left? _____
_____

Week 38: Journey Through Malachi

Malachi was the prophet whose name means "my messenger" and he has some words of wisdom for the people of God: "be true to the God who has always been true to you." They want to know how they have been unfaithful and he tells them, point by point. They were going through the motions, but their hearts were not in it. God is the God of many, many chances.

PEEK AT MY PRAYER

Good Morning Father, help us to always put our hearts into everything that we do, mindful that this is the part of us that You see clearly. Please and thank You! In Jesus' name I pray. Amen!

✝✝✝

Questions Week 38 – Malachi Chapters 1-4

1. What does the LORD say about Jacob and Esau? _____
_____

2. What is God's complaint about the offerings of the priests? _____
_____

3. How have the people robbed God and what is the solution to being blessed? _____
_____

4. Who will be sent before the great and dreadful day of the LORD?_____
_____
_____

Weeks 38 – 39: Journey Through Matthew

Welcome to the first book of the New Testament, the book of Matthew. Matthew was one of four gospel writers who gives an account of the life of Jesus.

Matthew was a Jewish tax collector called by Jesus, and became one of the 12 apostles. He shows Jesus as the son of David and as the one who fulfills Old Testament writings. Through Matthew, you will hear the Sermon on the Mount; you will learn the Lord's Prayer, and you will get a glimpse of future events.

Dear Lord, thank You for the privilege of being able to come to Your mighty throne of grace. Help us Father to never take You or Your Word for granted. Please and thank You! In Jesus' name I pray. Amen!

Journey Through Matthew

Questions Week 38 – Matthew Chapters 1-10

1. How many generations were there from Abraham to Jesus? _____

2. What were the gifts of the magi/wise men? _____

3. Who baptized Jesus and what was said from heaven? _____

4. Who were the first apostles called by Jesus? _____

5. What does Jesus say about the pure in heart and the peacemakers? _____

6. Describe the gate that leads to destruction and the gate that leads to life. _____

7. When He had called them, what did Jesus give to the 12 apostles? _____

Journey Through the Bible in Eleven Months

Questions Week 39 – Matthew Chapters 11-28

1. What is the sin that will not be forgiven? _____
   _____

2. What does Jesus say about our words on the Day of Judgment? _____
   _____

3. According to Jesus, where is a prophet without honor? _____
   _____

4. How was John the Baptist killed? _____
   _____

5. How many were fed with the five loaves and two fishes? _____

6. Why did Jesus heal the Canaanite woman's daughter when He said that He came only for the lost sheep of the house of Israel? _____
   _____

7. Jesus called the teachers of the law and the Pharisees hypocrites. He says that they tithe, but neglect the weightier matters of the law. What are these matters? _____
   _____

8. Give three of the seven signs of the end of the world (time). _____
   _____

9. In the Garden of Gethsemane just before His arrest, what was Jesus' prayer? ____
   _____

10. What message did Pilate's wife send to him concerning Jesus? _____
    _____
    _____
    _____

Weeks 39 – 40: Journey Through Mark

Mark was the son of a wealthy woman named Mary, and he writes to the Gentile reader. His approach to the gospel is different than Matthew's. While Matthew gives a detailed account of the genealogy of Jesus, Mark focuses more on the servitude of Jesus. He starts with the baptism of Jesus, by John the Baptist, and continues with the picture of our Lord, as the servant. He tells of the feeding of the 5,000, but not the Sermon on the Mount. And just like the other gospel writers, Mark shows us the love that the Savior has for each one of us.

PEEK AT MY PRAYER

Thank You Father, for the overwhelming love that You have for each one of us. Help us to always know that You are the one who has a plan for each of our lives. Please and thank You! In Jesus' name I pray. Amen!

Questions Week 39 – Mark Chapters 1-8

1. Why wouldn't Jesus let the devils speak once He had driven them out? _____

2. The scribes and Pharisees asked why Jesus ate with the tax collectors and sinners. What did He say? _____

3. Who did Jesus say was His mother and his brethren? _____

4. What did Jesus say to Jairus' little girl when He took her by the hand? _____

5. Jesus said it wasn't what went into a man, but what came out of him that defiled him. What was He referring to? _____

Journey Through the Bible in Eleven Months

Questions Week 40 – Mark Chapters 9-16

1. What answer does Jesus give when He asks how hard it is for those with riches to enter the kingdom of God? _____

2. What did the people shout when Jesus rode into the city on a colt? _____

3. What does Jesus say are the most important and greatest of the commandments? _____

4. For what reason will the Lord shorten the days of the affliction (doom and destruction)? _____

5. What signal did Judas give when he brought the chief priests to Jesus to betray Him? _____

6. Who was forced to carry the cross of Jesus? _____

7. At the ninth hour, what did Jesus cry out from the cross? _____

8. Who was the prominent member of the council that asked for the body of Jesus? _____

SO WHY THEN DO WE PRAY?

From a distance, he reminded her of her son. The way that he walked, the swing of his arms, and his height were some of the obvious things that were similar to her son. Her husband felt the same way and confirmed her thoughts. "He is just like your son," he said. "He looks like him. He acts like him; he even sounds like him." In her heart, without even knowing him, she knew that he had a nervous energy.

She got up early every morning and had coffee on the patio. This is when she would see him walking the length of the yard. He had to be doing something, anything; there was restlessness about him that she saw. This nervous energy had him looking for something to do, something to clean-up, or fix-up, or burn-up, just something to do.

He had a drug problem, and it was a bad one. This she learned from her husband. She knew how it was to have a bad drug problem. This is when something took a hold of her heart, and she began to pray for this man that she didn't even know. Compassion for another person was easy for her. Every morning she spoke his name to the Lord. She put him on the altar before the Holy God of her life, just as with her children and grandchildren. Tears for the man ran down her cheeks when she prayed. She had never spoken a word to him.

She confided in her husband when she found out that his family had put him out. "The Lord has placed a burden on my heart for him, and I have been praying for him." She prayed for him not only because he reminded her of her son, but also because she knew his bondage, and knew it well. She had been in the same lifestyle, caught up in some really bad stuff. But it was more than that; God Himself had put this burden on her, and she could do no less than what He required of her. But still she asked Him, "Father, why is this man that I don't even know, that I have never spoken to, someone that You have me praying for? I don't understand; he doesn't even know that I'm praying for him." And very quietly and softly she sensed the answer more then she heard it. "My precious, precious child, when you had no concept or idea of Who I Am, someone that you didn't know, someone that you had never spoken to, was obedient to me and prayed for you." She closed her eyes to stop the flow of tears that were running down her face and said, "Thank You Father."

Weeks 40 – 41: Journey Through Luke

This third writer of the gospel was a doctor named Luke. He was not an eyewitness to the life of Jesus, but he did interview those that were. He had an uncanny ability to put down into words all that he learned. He put much detail into his account of the gospel. He was a Gentile believer and what we would call an "olden day" evangelist. He puts information into his accounting that we don't get from the other writers. We learn from him, that Jesus and John the Baptist were cousins, and we get a glimpse into a portion of Jesus' childhood. From what we gather from Luke, it is safe to say that one of his gifts from the Lord was to accurately write.

Dear God, thank You for such a wonderful journey through Your precious Word. Help us to apply as much as we can to always stay the course. Please and thank You! In Jesus' name I pray. Amen!

Journey Through Luke

Questions Week 40 – Luke Chapters 1-20

1. What does the angel say about himself after he told Zechariah that he would be a father?

2. What happened when Elizabeth heard Mary's greeting and what did she say?

3. When the people thought that John the Baptist could be the Christ, what did he say to them?

4. When the disciples of John were sent to Jesus to ask if He was the one, or should they be looking for someone else, what did He say?

5. What was the man's name that had many demons?

6. What does Jesus say about kingdoms and houses that are divided against themselves?

7. Why is there joy in the presence of the angels of God?

8. In order to enter the kingdom of God, how are we to receive it?

Journey Through the Bible in Eleven Months

Questions Week 41 – Luke Chapters 21-24

1. Jesus knew that His time was near. What was His prayer and plea to the Father?

2. What did Jesus say to the betrayer as He approached him in the garden?

3. On what charge was Jesus being tried?

4. What did the sign read that was placed above Jesus' head on the cross?

5. According to Luke's gospel, what happened between the sixth and the ninth hour?

Week 41: Journey Through John

The writer of this book is John, one of the 12 disciples. He writes in the third person, referring to himself as "the disciple that Jesus loved."

When I became a child of the Lord's, this is the book that I was encouraged to read. It shows us the Holy Jesus, the undeniable Son of God, the Savior of the world. We see and recognize that deity was among mankind. We learn that He is God in the flesh, and that the world was made by Him.

Chapter 17 is truly the Lord's Prayer, prayed for each one of us in a garden called Gethsemane. In His prayer, you will certainly realize His love for each one of us. You will witness the fervency with which He prays. He was going to the cross, but took the time to lift us up to the Father. Now that's love, pure love.

PEEK AT MY PRAYER

Thank You, Father, for the love that You had for us before the foundations were ever put into place. Bless us to realize that love and to always walk in it. Please and thank You! In Jesus' name I pray. Amen!

Journey Through the Bible in Eleven Months

Questions Week 41 – John Chapters 1-21

1. Explain in the beginning was the Word. _____

2. Why was John the Baptist sent from God? _____

3. Where was Jesus when He performed His first miracle and what was that miracle? _____

4. How much does God love the whole world? _____

5. How will the true worshippers worship God? _____

6. Who does Jesus tell the Samaritan woman that He is? _____

7. When Jesus declares Himself the bread of life, what does He say about anyone who comes and believes in Him? _____

8. Who is the Good Shepherd and what does He do for His sheep? _____

Journey Through John

9. Why did Jesus weep? _____
   _____
   _____

10. Jesus says to the disciples that for your own good He is going away. When He goes away, who will He send? _____

11. What was Jesus' reply to Pilate when Pilate told Jesus he has the power either to free Him or to crucify Him? _____
    _____
    _____

    Extra Credit: In what chapter does Jesus fervently pray and intercede for all of us (the church)? _____

Week 42: Journey Through Acts

The book of Acts was written by Luke, the doctor who also wrote the gospel under his same name. In this book we see the early church and how it grew. It is an extension of what Jesus came to do, to show love to a dying world. You will be a witness to the Holy Spirit filling the people with His presence and His power. Peter and John continue the spread of the gospel even though there was much opposition and persecution. You will meet Stephen, a man full of God's grace and power, who was the first person martyred for his beliefs. Also, you will witness the conversion of one of the most outspoken opponents of the church. Take the time to realize that this is the forward motion of the church.

Thank You Father for Your love, Your mercy, and Your grace. Help us to be worthy to push forward and expand Your church. Walk us through every day, giving us the opportunities to tell someone the good news. Please and thank You! In Jesus' name I do pray. Amen!

Journey Through Acts

Questions Week 42 – Acts Chapters 1-28

1. On what day was the church born and the Holy Ghost given? _____

2. When the people heard the truth about who Jesus was, they were cut to the heart and asked what they should do. What did Peter tell them? _____

3. What sin were Ananias and Sapphira guilty of? _____

4. Who was Stephen and why was he stoned to death? What were his last words? _____

5. Who was at Stephen's death and what did he do to the church? _____

6. How was Saul converted? _____

7. Which of the apostles was the first to be martyred? _____

8. Why didn't Paul want John Mark on the second missionary journey, and how did this affect the journey? _____

125

Journey Through the Bible in Eleven Months

9. What was the character of the Bereans and what made them believe Paul? _____
   _____
   _____
   _____

10. How long was Paul in Rome and what did he do there? _____
    _____
    _____

Who Was Paul?

Paul, whose Jewish name was Saul, was a Pharisee, and as a Pharisee he considered himself expert in the law. He was very educated, and I have to believe that he loved God with all his heart, but he did not want to accept the changes that Jesus brought. Saul was loyal to what he considered to be the truth that Christ followers were to be destroyed. His zeal and fervency for his truth pushed him to do some terrible things toward Christians whom he hated. He had letters from the governing authorities to destroy the early church.

We have all known people who were adamant and compassionate about something that they believed was right, but were completely wrong. Saul was that person and the worst persecutor of the early church. He sincerely trusted that he was defending the God whom he loved. He was present at the stoning death of Stephen, a righteous man. He had Christians dragged out of their homes and put into prison. He was filled with rage against the Disciples of Christ.

But one day on his quest against Christians, he was "blinded by the light," the light of Christ himself. You see, like some of us, he was at a point in his life where God stepped in and showed him the error of his ways. So, he heard the truth, he accepted the truth, he began to live the truth and he went on to teach and encourage the truth. Saul's name was changed to Paul. He fell in love with the star of the gospels. He went on to write many of the epistles/letters that make up the New Testament.

The bottom line: Saul/Paul was just a sinner (chief, in his own words) saved by grace that changed his world. I, for one, look forward to meeting this man whose life brought glory to God.

Week 43: Journey Through Romans

This book is, in fact, a letter, also known as an epistle. It was written by Paul to the church in Rome. His intention is to go to Rome to minister there, and so he sent this letter to make known his plans to visit. In this letter, he commends the people for their great faith. He speaks of the holiness of God and the love of God for them. He explains to them that grace is a very precious gift and they would all do well to embrace it wholeheartedly. His encouraging words show us the love that he had for the church in Rome.

Good Morning Father, as we journey through Your most holy and precious Word, pull each one of us a little closer to You so that we might know You better. We do love You. Please and thank You! In Jesus' name I pray. Amen!

Journey Through Romans

Questions Week 43 – Romans Chapters 1-16

1. Why does Paul say he is not ashamed of the gospel? _____
   _____

2. Paul tells of the righteousness of God. What is this righteousness? _____
   _____

3. What did David say about the man to whom God imputes righteousness apart from works? _____
   _____

4. Through hope that does not make ashamed, how has God poured out His love to our hearts? _____

5. What was the result of the offence of one that affected all men, and what was the result of the righteousness of one that affected all men? _____
   _____
   _____

6. What is Paul persuaded of in regard to the love of God? _____
   _____
   _____

7. How does Paul assure us that not only the Jews, but also the Gentiles have been called? _____
   _____

8. What does the heart and mouth have to do in order to be justified and saved? _____

9. Paul beseeches us by God's mercy to do what? _____
   _____
   _____

10. Everything written in the past was written to teach us what? _____
    _____
    _____

Journey Through the Bible in Eleven Months

Week 43: Journey Through 1 Corinthians

This is another letter written by Paul, to the people in the church in Corinth. Now the city of Corinth was a very sinful place, with the inhabitants doing every unimaginable thing. Paul writes to the church, because it has become apparent that sin was creeping into the church. Since he preached the gospel there, he has a concern for them. He expresses his disappointment over the things being done in the church, but wisely, he points to Christ as the example that they should follow.

Dear God, thank You so much for Your Word. Help us each to always do that which will please You. Show us where we falter and point us to Jesus. Please and thank You! In Jesus' name I pray. Amen!

Journey Through 1 Corinthians

Questions Week 43 – 1 Corinthians Chapters 1-16

1. According to Paul, what did God choose over wisdom and might? _____
   _____
   _____

2. What does Paul say we are to do when we are reviled, persecuted, and defamed?
   _____
   _____
   _____

3. If a woman's husband dies, on what condition is she free to remarry? _____
   _____

4. What does Paul mean when he states he has become all things to all men? _____
   _____

5. What should we all do before we eat of the bread and drink from the cup of the Lord?
   _____
   _____

6. Name the qualities of what charity (love) is and what it is not. _____
   _____

7. What is the last enemy that Christ will destroy? _____

Journey Through the Bible in Eleven Months

JUST A SINNER

A letter to the church: You hurt me so bad,
That when I walked out, I was confused and sad.

The place that I was in just couldn't be my life.
I was tired of the sin, the struggle, the strife.

My life hasn't been pretty, and it hasn't been kind.
I was just looking for a place that I could unwind.

So, I came to your service, I was truly a mess.
I was looking for compassion, just needed to rest.

I looked at your faces, just needed a smile.
You turned away, but I sat for a while.

This is what I know and this is what I saw.
As soon as you saw me you threw up a wall.

I knew my skirt was too short and my shirt was too tight,
But the way you treated me, it just wasn't right.

I could have been an angel sent from above,
But I was just a sinner looking for love.

You looked this way, and that way; wouldn't look in my eyes,
I just bent my head down and I started to cry.

The pain in my life is what brought me there,
And if Jesus is like you, then He really don't care.

I prayed, "God, if they are like You,
Then I'm gonna continue to do what I do."

They want to be seen by the powers that be,
I guess that's not You, and I know it's not me.

JUST A SINNER (Cont.)

So, give me a reason why I should not go.
I thought this was the place Your love would show.

He said, "Child, just keep your eyes on Me.
There is something here I want you to see."

Then I saw one that was shining so bright,
A nod of their head made it alright.

I needed to see that one that was real.
They gave me hope, I started to heal.

The one that was shining was nicer than nice.
And they are the reason I'd come back twice.

Just because of the light that is there.
I know that He's good; I know that He's fair.

So, please be the one that lights up the room.
Even I, just a sinner, know He's coming back soon.

Week 44: Journey Through 2 Corinthians

Since the writing of 1 Corinthians, the church has grown but not without pain and controversy. It is believed that another letter was written that contained some harsh and hurtful things. Paul wrote what was necessary to turn the people back to a loving God. With the writing of 2 Corinthians, the church has repented and turned back to the grace and love of God. This letter is very loving and kind in that Paul explains some truths regarding the Lord. He very much wants the church to have an eagerness and enthusiasm for the things pertaining to God.

Good Morning Father, thank You for the ones who are on this journey. Help us dear Lord, to hear You through Your Word, and to apply it to our hearts. Please and thank You! In Jesus' name I pray. Amen!

Journey Through 2 Corinthians

Questions Week 44 – 2 Corinthians Chapters 1-13

1. If any has caused grief and is worthy of punishment, what should we do for that person?

2. God has made us sufficient and able as ministers. Please explain.

3. Why must we all appear before the judgment seat of Christ one day?

4. What does godly sorrow produce and what does worldly sorrow produce?

5. When Paul pled with the Lord three times to take away the thorn in his flesh, what did God say?

Journey Through the Bible in Eleven Months

MY GOD WHO IS COLORLESS

Maybe I'm not the one who should be up here speakin'.
My momma who was wise, to me she was always teachin'.

That prejudices been around since the beginning of days,
And the enemy will use it in so many ways.

He has been around since before the great flood.
"Your battle," she said, "Is not flesh, is not blood."

He will put nation against nation,
And black against white,
But really my daughter, it's dark against light.

It's a spiritual battle. A war you can't see.
The chaos and confusion won't let you be free.

She said, "We have to get along no matter the cost.
When we don't keep our focus, there's a chance we'll get lost."

So, let's not get caught up in the color of skin.
My God who is colorless will make sure that we win.

Hate can only be conquered by a love that is real.
Let's all start to show it; let's all start to heal.

True love was nailed to a cross and pierced in its side.
And it never stopped loving the whole worldwide.

We must not give in to this thing that's called sin.
The battle is the Lord's, you should trust that He will win.

Because that same love rose up for me and for you.
He did it for us all, for the red, yellow, and blue.

Week 44: Journey Through Galatians

Paul wrote to the church in Galatia in response to false teachings. There were certain Christian Jews called the Judaizers that were teaching that faith was not enough and that works were necessary for salvation. So, this letter from Paul addressed the issues, and he set them straight on circumcision, the law, and faith. He made it clear that circumcision did not save; that Jesus had fulfilled the law, and that faith in Jesus alone is what sanctified and justified their lives. And because of their belief in Jesus, they were saved.

Dear God, let us always hold on to the facts and not anything that tries to change what we have been taught and believe, that Jesus is Lord. Please and thank You! In Jesus' name I pray. Amen!

Questions Week 44 – Galatians Chapters 1-6

1. Who is Paul referring to when he says let him be accursed? _____

2. Paul and Peter were tasked with preaching the gospel to two different groups of people. Who were they? _____

3. According to Paul, who are the children of Abraham? _____

4. What is the fruit of the spirit? _____

Week 44: Journey Through Ephesians

This letter written by Paul is sent to the church in Ephesus. He very plainly tells them God's reason and purpose for the church. He reminds them of the grace of God, and our predestination, before the foundations of the world, by God, and that Christ is and always will be the head of each one of us (the church). And as that body of Christ, we can do all things through Him. We are commanded to love at all times.

Dear Father, we love You more and more every day. Please continue to reveal Your truths to not only our minds, but to our hearts. Please and thank You! In Jesus' name I pray. Amen!

Journey Through Ephesians

Questions Week 44 – Ephesians Chapters 1-6

1. What happens when we hear the word of truth and believe? _____
_____
_____

2. What is the gift of God of having been saved? _____

3. What is happening to us as we speak the truth in love? _____
_____

4. How are husbands to love their wives and why? _____
_____
_____

5. What is the whole armor of God and explain how each part works? _____
_____
_____
_____
_____
_____
_____
_____

Journey Through the Bible in Eleven Months

Week 44: Journey Through Philippians

And still another letter from Paul. He had a very loving relationship with the church at Philippi. They accepted the gospel from the very beginning and with this letter, Paul encourages them to grow, grow, grow. Grow in their wisdom, grow in their knowledge, and to grow in the love of the Lord. He reminds them to always have peace, and to always stand firm in their faith. (We do well to follow these pearls of truth.)

Good Morning Father, Help each one of us to always grow in our faith in You. Teach us those things that we need, in order to accomplish Your will for our lives. Please and thank You! In Jesus' name I pray. Amen!

✝✝

Questions Week 44 – Philippians Chapters 1-4

1. What was Paul's prayer for the church at Philippi? _____

_____
_____
_____
_____

2. How does Paul describe the enemies of the cross of Christ? _____

_____

3. Paul tells us to think on some things. What are these things? _____

_____
_____
_____

Week 45: Journey Through Colossians

This letter was written to the church at Colossae, from the Apostle Paul. While he did not play a major role in bringing the gospel to them, he was proud of the way they grabbed a hold to it. He is an encourager at heart, and this is what he does for them. He lets them know that he is praying for their faith to grow in the knowledge of Christ. And as he encourages them, he lets them know that they should also encourage each other.

Good Morning Father, how far we have come. Help us dear Lord to keep what we learn deep in our hearts and to live a life in which You are proud. Please and thank You! In Jesus' name I pray. Amen!

✝✝

Questions Week 45 – Colossians Chapters 1-4

1. Who preached the gospel of truth to the Colossians? _____

2. Paul had great conflict for those at Colossae, Laodicea, and for those he had not met. What was the purpose of his conflict? _____

3. As the Word of Christ dwells in us, how should we teach and admonish one another?

Week 45: Journey Through 1 Thessalonians

Paul is so thankful for the Thessalonians, that he is moved to write this letter and express his love towards them. He encourages their faith in the Lord, and their love, one towards another. He gives them insight into future events, namely the day of the Lord. Jesus will come for His people; therefore, His people should always be ready for His appearing.

Dear God, help us to always be looking for Your coming for us, Your people. We love You so much. Please and thank You! In Jesus' name I pray. Amen!

Journey Through 1 Thessalonians

Questions Week 45 – 1 Thessalonians Chapters 1-5

1. What does Paul say is continually remembered concerning the Thessalonians?

2. What are the Thessalonians told to make their study/ambition, and why?

3. How will the day of the Lord come?

4. What is God's will for us in Christ Jesus?

Journey Through the Bible in Eleven Months

Week 45: Journey Through 2 Thessalonians

Paul sent this second letter to the church at Thessalonica, because there was confusion about the coming of the Lord. Some believed that the judgments of God had started, because of the troubles in their lives. Paul seeks to ease and comfort them. He wants them to understand that they should always be working in the ministry no matter what. He tells them some specifics concerning the day of the Lord, and again he encourages them to live their faith out.

PEEK AT MY PRAYER

Good Morning, Father, please show each of us how to live according to Your will, even when things are not as they should be. Please and thank You! In Jesus' name I pray. Amen!

✝✝

Questions Week 45 – 2 Thessalonians Chapters 1-3

1. What punishment awaits those who don't know God and do not obey the gospel of Jesus?

_____
_____
_____
_____

2. The day of Christ the Lord will not come until certain things happen. What are they?

_____
_____
_____

Week 45: Journey Through 1 Timothy

This is the first of two letters written by Paul, to Timothy. He wants this young preacher to know how to shepherd God's people. He encourages him to be a good example to his congregation, to fight the good fight, to hold onto his faith, and to always have a good conscience.

Hello Father, as we study Your Word, we will make it a point to live according to it. Help us every day Lord to please You, and when we fail, forgive us. Please and thank You! In Jesus' name I pray. Amen!

✝✝

Questions Week 45 – 1 Timothy Chapters 1-6

1. What is Paul's will for men everywhere to do? _____
   _____
   _____

2. What are the qualifications of the bishop (pastor) of the church? _____
   _____
   _____
   _____

3. What is the great mystery of godliness? _____
   _____
   _____

4. What is the snare of the rich and root of all evil? _____
   _____

Week 45: Journey Through 2 Timothy

Again, we see the apostle Paul penning a letter to Timothy. Paul is writing this letter from behind prison walls. Paul regards Timothy as his son in the ministry and just wants to encourage him. He writes and lovingly instructs that Timothy be a solider of Christ, to study God's Word, to be ready to preach, rebuke when necessary, and to always love the people of God.

Dear Father, let us be an example to others of Your overwhelming love. Lead and guide us every single day of our lives. Please and thank You! In Jesus' name I pray. Amen!

✝✝✝

Questions Week 45 – 2 Timothy Chapters 1-4

1. What kind of spirit should we have instead of a spirit of fear? _____
   _____
   _____

2. Timothy is encouraged to study. Why? _____
   _____
   _____
   _____

3. Where does all scripture come from and what is it useful for? _____
   _____
   _____

LISA IS HER NAME

Each and every day as my knees hit the floor
I say, "Good Morning Father," and He opens the door.

I run to His throne and put my head on His knee.
I always can feel His great love for me.

The tears start to fall before I utter a word.
Everything I tell Him, He's already heard.

Father, today I'm praying for my child.
She's just like me and I used to be wild.

I loved my child that just wouldn't do right,
And I knew in the spirit, I could put up a fight.

Hers is a voice for a while I hadn't heard.
Please dear God be true to Your Word.

I'm pleading for this girl that You gave to me.
Lord, break that hold and please set her free!

I'm praying this prayer that's hard to say,
But whatever it takes Father, bring her back this way.

And while on my knees, my phone it did ring,
And when I heard her voice, my heart it did sing.

You see, this is my first, and Lisa is her name,
And for the kingdom of God, her life I do claim.

"Mom," she said with tears in her eyes.
"I'm being arrested," and she began to cry.

My heart seemed to drop deep in my chest;
You know for your children you want only the best.

And if you believe that the Lord hears your voice,
Then pray for your kids cuz you don't have a choice.

And they'll hurt you, and hurt you, and hurt you some more,
But never stop praying, keep your knees on the floor.

I believe that one day she'll be praising His name;
Her testimony will be mighty and heaven her aim.

Now she will call me more than before,
And I'm still praying with my knees on the floor.

Week 46: Journey Through Titus

Titus was a man of whom Paul was very proud. This letter is instructive and encouraging. Paul lays out the guidelines of what a healthy church should look like. He writes that Titus must be stern with those who were rebellious and those who were troublemakers. But he wants him to encourage those who love the Lord. He is to teach them, so that they may in turn teach others. Paul reminds Titus of God's great love and great grace. In short, this letter lets all of us know that we are to always do what is right.

PEEK AT MY PRAYER

Good Morning Lord, thank You for instruction on how to live in a world that seems to get worse and worse. Continue to keep each one of us on our journey through life. Please and thank You! In Jesus' name I pray. Amen!

✞✞✞

Questions Week 46 – Titus Chapters 1-3

1. How are the older women in the church to act and teach the younger women?

   _____
   _____
   _____

2. What was Titus told to remind the people of? _____

   _____
   _____
   _____

Week 46: Journey Through Philemon

This is a personal letter, written to a man named Philemon, on behalf of a runaway servant named Onesimus. Paul starts the letter by thanking God for the good and godly man that Philemon is. He then encourages him with the news that Onesimus is a changed man, and that he is coming home. He pleads with him to treat Onesimus as he would a brother of the faith, and to count his conversion as gain for the kingdom.

PEEK AT MY PRAYER

Dear God, thank You for those things in our lives that help us to grow and see You more clearly. Help us to grow through all the trials and heartaches that come our way. Please and thank You! In Jesus' name I pray. Amen!

Questions Week 46 – Philemon

1. What is the name of the runaway slave that Paul is sending back to Philemon?
_____

Journey Through the Bible in Eleven Months

Week 46: Journey Through Hebrews

While it is unclear who wrote the book of Hebrews, we do know that it is fitting for all believers everywhere. It gives a history of God's people after leaving Egypt and it gives us truths about how to live a life pleasing to God. We see Christ as our high priest, as we are encouraged to take hold of faith, and to live by that same faith. Truly this book sent to the Hebrews gives all of God's people instructions for living a godly and peaceful life.

Dear God, thank You for the way You keep us day by day. Help us to appreciate that every part of our lives is precious to You. Please and thank You! In Jesus' name I pray. Amen!

Journey Through Hebrews

Questions Week 46 – Hebrews Chapters 1-13

1. What is another name for angels and why are they sent? _____

2. How does the writer of Hebrews describe the Word of God? _____

3. How are we to approach the throne of God and why? _____

4. How does Melchizedek, king of Salem, represent the high priest (Jesus)? _____

5. How did Jesus enter the most holy place? _____

6. What is faith? _____

7. What should we do since we are surrounded by a great cloud of witnesses? _____

8. Why are we told not to forget to entertain strangers? _____

Journey Through the Bible in Eleven Months

Week 46: Journey Through James

This letter was written by the brother of our Lord Jesus. It went out to "the 12 tribes which are scattered," or to the Jews. James writes beautifully about faith and wisdom. Without faith, it is impossible to please God. When we need wisdom, all we have to do is ask. James makes it clear that we are to endure, with patience, as we look for the soon return of the Lord.

Good Morning Father, today we do ask that not only do You increase our faith, but give to us wisdom that we lack, and patience to wait on You. Please and thank You! In Jesus' name I pray. Amen!

Journey Through James

Questions Week 46 – James Chapters 1-5

1. What are we to do when we lack wisdom? _____
   _____

2. Why is the man blessed who endures temptation? _____
   _____
   _____
   _____

3. Describe the wisdom that comes from heaven. _____
   _____
   _____
   _____

4. What have we done when we turn a sinner from the error of his ways? _____
   _____
   _____

Week 47: Journey Through 1 Peter

The writer of this book is the apostle, Peter. He tells of an inheritance that is incorruptible and that will never fade away. Peter gives instructions to all of us on how to live a life full of grace. This grace is true and will get us through every day of our journey. He encourages us to not falter or faint, but to know when hard times come, the grace of God will get us through.

Dear God, thank You for those that have come this far in this journey through Your precious Word. Help each of us to not only read Your Word, but to also live Your Word. Knowing that in every circumstance of our lives, You are there. Please and thank You! In Jesus' name I pray. Amen!

✝✝

Questions Week 47 – 1 Peter Chapters 1-5

1. How should the trials of our faith encourage us? _____
   _____
   _____

2. In what ways are the eyes, ears, and the face of the Lord turned to? _____
   _____
   _____

3. How are we to use the gifts that we have received? _____

4. Since God gives grace to the humble, how should we react to that grace? _____
   _____

Week 47: Journey Through 2 Peter

In this second writing of Peter, the point that he makes is that there are false teachers, false doctrines, and a false light. We should be aware of people who would try and convince us of things that we know are just not true. God has a place prepared for such people. He will not let anyone or anything take us from Him. He is our protector.

Good Morning Father, and thank You, for life, for peace, and for Your love that is overwhelming. Help us all to do better in our journey on this earth. Please and thank You! In Jesus' name I pray. Amen!

✝✝

Questions Week 47 – 2 Peter Chapters 1-3

1. If we are eager to make our calling and election sure, what is the promise? _____
   _____
   _____

2. Describe Lot and how he felt living in the cities of Sodom and Gomorrah. _____
   _____
   _____

3. According to the Word, what are the present heavens and earth reserved for? _____
   _____
   _____

Week 47: Journey Through 1 John

It is believed that this book was written by the Apostle John. He encourages us to always walk in the light because our Father is light. He encourages us to always love because our Father is love. He encourages us to be righteous because our Father is righteous. And he encourages us to confess our sins because our Father will forgive.

Hello Father, this is the day that You have made; help each one of us to be thankful and glad in it. Please and thank You! We do love you! In Jesus' name I pray. Amen!

Journey Through 1 John

Questions Week 47 – 1 John Chapters 1-5

1. What does the Bible say about those who claim to be without sin and those who confess their sin? _____
   _____
   _____

2. How do we know who the children of God are and who the children of the devil are?
   _____
   _____

3. How do we know what the love is and how do we show it to others? _____
   _____
   _____

4. How did God show/manifest His love toward us? _____
   _____
   _____

5. What is the confidence that we have in approaching God? _____
   _____
   _____

Week 47: Journey Through 2 John

This letter, written by John, seems to be a personal letter to a lady and her children. John commends them for walking in truth, commands that they love one another, and cautions them to be aware of the false teachers. John shows pride towards this lady and her love of God. (We, as the church, should strive to be just like this "lady.")

Hello Father, how can we be pleasing to You today? Please show us exactly what You want from each one of us, so that we can be what You intend us to be. Please and thank You! In Jesus' name I pray! Amen!

✝✝✝

Questions Week 47 – 2 John

1. What does John say about love to the elect lady and her children? _____
_____
_____

Week 47: Journey Through 3 John

This third letter written by John is to his very good friend Gaius. John is happy to hear of the hospitality and grace that Gaius shows towards traveling ministers. He mentions a self-centered man, Diotrephes, who is a bad reflection of how a man of God should be. John encourages Gaius to continue to always do what is right and to continue to be faithful to the truth.

Good Morning Father, today we give You our hearts for safe keeping. Help us dear Lord to let You mold them to always do what is right in Your sight. Please and thank You! In Jesus' name I pray. Amen!

✟✟

Questions Week 47 – 3 John

1. Why does John have great joy over Gaius? _____
_____
_____
_____
_____

Week 47: Journey Through Jude

This short letter was written by Jude, the half-brother of Jesus. It is a letter to all believers everywhere. He wanted them to be aware of the false, non-believing teachers, who were slipping into the churches. He describes them as being selfish, with their own agenda, greedy, prideful, rebellious, and having no respect for authority. Jude exhorts the believers to keep the faith, to pray in the spirit, and to stay in God's love.

Dear God, we know that there are those who would try to shake our faith, so we need You to help us to recognize them and to stay true to You. Please and thank You! In Jesus' name I pray. Amen!

✝✝

Questions Week 47 – Jude

1. Who is Jude and who is he speaking to? _____
   _____
   _____

2. What does Jude say about certain men, those that believe not, and the angels that rebelled?
   _____
   _____
   _____

Week 48: Journey Through Revelation

The book of Revelation was written by the Apostle John. He was in exile on an island called Patmos during the time of the writing of this book. It reveals Jesus as the risen Savior of the world.

In this book, there are things that will be easy to understand, and some things not so easy to understand. And since our God has made us all different, we will all have our own opinions and thoughts as to what this book means. Just read it!

- Is it a book about the past and what has already been?
- Is it a book about the future and what is to come?
- Is it a book about what is happening in our world right now?
- Or can it be about the past, about the future, and about right now?

One thing is for certain, it is a book of prophecy and the revelation of our Lord and Savior Jesus the Christ!

PEEK AT MY PRAYER

Most holy and mighty God, I do come before Your wonderful throne of grace, on behalf of these who have come to the end of the journey through Your Word. Bless abundantly as only You can. Please and thank You! In Jesus' Holy and mighty name I do pray! Amen!

Journey Through the Bible in Eleven Months

Questions Week 48 – Revelation Chapters 1-22

1. Who is the book of Revelation about, who was it made known to, and what is the promise to those who read and hear the prophecy of this book? _____

2. Jesus has a message to seven churches. What are the promises to him who overcomes?

3. What did the 24 elders have on? _____

4. Describe the four beasts around the throne and what do they never stop saying?

5. Why is John weeping, and what is it that stops him? _____

6. Briefly describe the six seals of Chapter 6, and the color associated with each of them.

Journey Through Revelation

7. The four angels were told not to harm the earth nor the sea until what was done?

   _____

   _____

8. What does the seventh seal usher in? _____

   _____

9. What does the flying angel call out during the fourth trumpet sound? _____

   _____

10. What is the name of the angel/king of the bottomless pit and what does his name mean?

    _____

    _____

11. Describe the eating of the little book. _____

    _____

    _____

12. Who will worship the beast? _____

    _____

    _____

13. Why do you think that the seven angels with the seven plagues are last? ____

    _____

    _____

14. In Chapter 19, what does the angel tell John to write? _____

    _____

    _____

15. How does Jesus say He is coming? _____

    _____

Journey Through the Bible in Eleven Months

I AM YOU AND YOU ARE ME

Please, let's not judge each other by the way that we look.
This is not important, so says the Book!

***I AM** not black or white, not Jewish or Chinese,*
*But if you look closely, **I AM** all of these.*

***I AM** not straight or gay, not a Muslim or a Mexican.*
*Please look a little closer, cuz you know that **I AM**.*

***I AM** that there widow that sits all alone.*
She looks out her windows. She stares at her phone.

Her life has been changed and to her it's not fair.
*Depression has set in, and with her **I AM** there.*

***I AM** the mother that lost her dear child,*
*And **I AM** the Saint that used to be wild.*

If she could have planned her child's life,
It would have been different, no struggles, no strife.

***I AM** the one, the one with no hope.*
***I AM** out on the street, the one who will do anything for dope.*

***I AM** the shake of a head that says, "Oh what a shame."*
*And **I AM** the plea that you'd ask me my name.*

***I AM** the cry from the child that was hurt.*
And I'm the one who did it in my green-striped shirt.

***I AM** the cancer that eats from within.*
*Please look at me; **I AM** the forgiveness of sin.*

***I AM** the wealthy and the poorest of poor,*
*And **I AM** the knock that opens the door.*

I AM YOU AND YOU ARE ME (Cont.)

I AM the pain of a shattered, broken heart,
And I AM the smile that brings a new start.

I AM the wicked, and the holy, the good and the bad.
I look in the mirror, and I AM happy and sad.

Please understand that I AM you and you are me,
And we are all a part of humanity.

We are the humanity that He saw in that cup,
And He did not waver; His life He gave up.

We are one of this, and this is all of we,
And I AM thankful to God for the chance to be free.

So, whenever we go out and see what we see,
Please dear God, show us how we can help me.

Precious Lord we are sorry for the way that we've been.
Forgive all our yesterdays, let us try this again!

ANSWERS

You are about to enter the **Answer Zone**. I used the King James Bible to answer the questions. However, please feel free to use other Bible versions and resources. Also, these are suggested answers to be used as guidelines for your study.

Please email me at **stl_granny05@hotmail.com** with any comments, questions, or if you would like to be a part of my ongoing book study.

Journey Through the Bible in Eleven Months

Answers for Week 1 – Genesis Chapters 1-25

1. First Day: light; Second Day: firmament-heaven; Third Day: dry land and plants; Fourth Day: sun, moon, and stars; Fifth Day: birds and sea creatures; Sixth Day: land animals and humans; Seventh Day: God rested. (Genesis 1:1-31; 2:1-3)
2. God saw that everything was very good. (Genesis 1:31)
3. (Genesis 2:24)
4. Cain, a tiller of the ground, and Abel, a keeper of sheep. (Genesis 4:1-2)
5. Enoch. (Genesis 5:24)
6. Because of the wickedness of man. (Genesis 6:5)
7. A bow in the clouds. (Genesis 9:13)
8. Abram. (Genesis 12:1-2)
9. Abram was 99 years old when God changed his name to Abraham because God made him a father of many nations. (Genesis 17:1, 5)
10. Every man child among Abraham shall be circumcised. (Genesis 17:10)
11. Isaac. (Genesis 22:2)
12. Isaac's wife's name was Rebekah, and her twin sons' names were Esau and Jacob. (Genesis 25:20-26)

Answers for Week 2 – Genesis Chapters 26-50

1. Jacob conspired with his mother to lie to his father Isaac in order to receive the blessings (birthright) from his twin brother, the firstborn son, Esau. (Genesis 27:10-19)
2. Jacob ran to Laban in Haran. (Genesis 27:43)
3. The names of Laban's two daughters are Leah, the older, and Rachel, the younger. (Genesis 29:16)
4. Laban tricked Jacob by giving his daughter Leah to him in marriage before his daughter Rachel. (Genesis 29:23)
5. Rachel died in childbirth, and the name of her two sons were Joseph and Benjamin. (Genesis 35:17-18, 24)

Answers

6. Joseph was the favorite son of Jacob, who gifted him with a coat of many colors. (Genesis 37:3)

7. Joseph's brother Judah convinced his other brothers to sell him to the Ishmeelites instead of killing him. (Genesis 37:26-27)

8. They were to bring their youngest brother, Benjamin. (Genesis 42:34)

9. Rueben, Simeon, Levi, Judah, Issachar, Zebulun, Gad, Asher, Joseph, Benjamin, Dan, and Naphtali. (Genesis 46:8-24)

Extra Credit Answer: He is from the tribe of Judah.

Answers for Week 3 – Exodus Chapters 1-20

1. Pharaoh's daughter paid wages to the Hebrew woman who was the baby's mother. (Exodus 2:7-9)

2. She named the baby Moses because she drew him out of the water. (Exodus 2:10b)

3. God told Moses to say I AM THAT I AM sent me unto you. (Exodus 3:14)

4. Aaron and Moses are from the tribe of Levi. (Exodus 6:19-20)

5. The ten plagues of Egypt are: 1) water becomes blood; 2) frogs covered the land; 3) lice, 4) swarms of flies; 5) disease on animals; 6) boils; 7) hail and fire; 8) locusts; 9) darkness; 10) death to the firstborn. (Exodus 7:14-11:5)

6. They marked their door posts with lamb's blood. (Exodus 12:1-7, 13)

7. He had Moses to stretch his hand over the sea causing the sea to go back by a strong east wind, and turned the sea into dry land, and the waters were divided. (Exodus 14:21)

8. Miriam, the prophetess. (Exodus 15:20)

9. Jethro, the priest of Midian was the father-in-law of Moses. He counseled Moses to select capable men and appoint them as rulers. (Exodus 18:1, 19-22)

10. Because they pertain to God. (Exodus 20:3-8)

11. Honor thy father and thy mother: that thy days may be long upon the land which the LORD thy God giveth thee. (Exodus 20:12)

Journey Through the Bible in Eleven Months

Answers for Week 4 – Exodus Chapters 21-40

1. The feast of unleavened bread, the feast of harvest, and the feast of ingathering. (Exodus 23:15-16)
2. Moses was up on Mount Sinai with God 40 days and 40 nights. (Exodus 24:18)
3. Pure gold. (Exodus 25:11)
4. Between the holy place and the most holy. (Exodus 26:33)
5. God. (Exodus 32:16)
6. When Moses approached the camp, and saw the calf and the dancing, he was angered, and threw the tablets breaking them into pieces. (Exodus 32:19)
7. Moses saw the back parts of God. (Exodus 33:23)
8. By providing a cloud over the tabernacle by day, and fire was on it by night. (Exodus 40:38)

Answers for Week 5 – Leviticus Chapters 1-27

1. A young bullock as a sin offering. (Leviticus 4:14)
2. For seven days. (Leviticus 8:33)
3. Aaron's two sons were Nadab and Abihu. They offered unauthorized fire before the LORD. So, the LORD caused the fire to consume them, and they died before the LORD. (Leviticus 10:1-2)
4. A woman was considered unclean after childbirth for seven days if it was a male child, and two weeks if it was a female child. (Leviticus 12:2-5)
5. For I the LORD your God am holy. (Leviticus 19:2)
6. The feast of the Passover and unleavened bread, the feast of first fruits, the feast of Pentecost, the feast of trumpets, the feast of the day of atonement, and the feast of tabernacles. (Leviticus 23:4-44)
7. God gave Moses all the commands on Mount Sinai. (Leviticus 27:34)

Answers

Answers for Week 6 – Numbers Chapters 1-18

1. Because God wanted all the male Israelites 20 years or older who were able to go forth to war in Israel. (Numbers 1:2-45)
2. The Levites were not numbered with the tribe to be able to fight because they were in charge of the tabernacle of Testimony. (Numbers 1:47-50)
3. The Nazarite was not to eat anything that comes from the grapevine; no razor may be used on his head; he must not go near a dead body. (Numbers 6:3-6)
4. Levites 25 years or older shall serve in the tabernacle. (Numbers 8:24) From the age of 50 they shall retire. (Numbers 8:25)
5. When Moses prayed to the LORD on behalf of the people, the LORD quenched the fire. (Numbers 11:2)
6. Quails from the sea. (Numbers 11:31)
7. Miriam became leprous, white as snow. (Numbers 12:10)
8. Only two, Joshua and Caleb. (Numbers 14:6-7)
9. Korah, Dathan, and Abiram. (Numbers 16:27) The earth opened its mouth and swallowed them. (Numbers 16:32)
10. The rod belonged to Aaron, and it sprouted, budded, blossomed, and produced almonds. (Numbers 17:8)

Answers for Week 7 – Numbers Chapters 19-36

1. Moses hit the rock twice instead of speaking to the rock as God commanded. Because of this, he would not go into the Promised Land. (Numbers 20:8-12)
2. Phinehas. (Numbers 25:11-12)
3. Joshua, the son of Nun. (Numbers 27:18)
4. All the women children who have not known a man. (Numbers 31:18)
5. Aaron was 123 years old when he died. (Numbers 33:39)
6. Canaan. (Numbers 34:2)
7. Every daughter who inherits land must marry someone in her father's tribal clan. (Numbers 36:8)

Journey Through the Bible in Eleven Months

Answers for Week 8 – Deuteronomy Chapters 1-17

1. That the LORD would increase them a thousand times and bless them as He promised. (Deuteronomy 1:10-11)
2. Because Caleb had wholly followed the LORD. (Deuteronomy 1:36)
3. The people heard the voice of God speaking out of the midst of the fire. (Deuteronomy 4:33)
4. But by every word that proceedeth out of the mouth of the LORD. (Deuteronomy 8:3)
5. He fell down before the LORD for 40 days and 40 nights, and he ate no bread and drank no water. (Deuteronomy 9:18)
6. That prophet must be put to death. (Deuteronomy 13:5)
7. The month was Abib because the LORD brought them out of Egypt by night. This is when the Passover was instituted. (Deuteronomy 16:1)
8. They shall be stoned to death. (Deuteronomy 17:5)

Answers for Week 9 – Deuteronomy Chapters 18-34

1. The LORD is their inheritance. (Deuteronomy 18:2)
2. He was free for one year to be with his wife. (Deuteronomy 24:5)
3. The third year is the year of tithing. (Deuteronomy 26:12)
4. Their clothes and shoes never wore out. (Deuteronomy 29:5)
5. In the side of the ark of the covenant. (Deuteronomy 31:26)
6. Mount Nebo. (Deuteronomy 32:49)
7. Moses was 120 years old when he died. (Deuteronomy 34:7)
8. The Israelites grieved for Moses 30 days. (Deuteronomy 34:8)
9. Genesis, Exodus, Leviticus, Numbers, and Deuteronomy

Answers

Answers for Week 10 – Joshua Chapters 1-24

1. Rahab. (Joshua 2:1b)
2. She asked the two spies that her family would be spared from death. (Joshua 2:13)
3. Israel crossed the Jordan on dry land because the LORD dried up the water. (Joshua 4:23)
4. The next day after they had eaten of the old corn of the land. (Joshua 5:12)
5. He was the captain of the LORD's host. He told Joshua to take off his shoes, for the place he was standing was holy. (Joshua 5:14-15)
6. The men marched around once for six days, and on the seventh day they marched around seven times, then the wall collapsed. (Joshua 6:3-20)
7. The sun stood still, and the moon stopped for about a day. (Joshua 10:12-13)
8. Thirty-one kings were defeated. (Joshua 12:24)
9. Caleb inherited Hebron because he wholly followed the LORD. (Joshua 14:14)
10. The cities of refuge were for anyone who had unintentionally or accidentally killed someone. (Joshua 20:3)
11. As a witness between us and you, and our generations after us. (Joshua 22:27-28)

Answers for Week 11 – Judges Chapters 1-21

1. The spirit of the LORD came upon Othniel, Caleb's younger brother, and he became Israel's judge. (Judges 3:9-10)
2. The name of the judge was Deborah. (Judges 4:4) She was a woman. (Judges 4:9)
3. Gideon started with 32,000 and ended up with only 300. (Judges 7:3-8)
4. The vow was whosoever comes out of his house first when he returned in victory, he would sacrifice as a burnt offering. His daughter came out to meet him. He kept his vow and she died a virgin. (Judges 11:31-39)
5. Samson. (Judges 13:24)
6. Delilah was his downfall. (Judges 16:4-22)
7. There was war because the tribe of Benjamin refused to deliver the men who had abused and killed the Levite concubine. (Judges 20:3-13)

Journey Through the Bible in Eleven Months

Answers for Week 11 – Ruth Chapters 1-4

1. Orpah and Ruth. (Ruth 1:4)
2. Ruth pleaded with Naomi to let her stay because she wanted to be amongst Naomi's people, and Naomi's God to be her God. (Ruth 1:16)
3. Boaz. (Ruth 4:1)
4. Obed who was the grandfather of David. (Ruth 4:22)

Answers for Week 12 – 1 Samuel Chapters 1-31

1. Samuel's mother was Hannah. (1 Samuel 1:20)
2. Four times. (1 Samuel 3:4-10)
3. She named the boy Ichabod, saying the glory has departed from Israel, for the ark of God has been captured. (1 Samuel 4:21-22)
4. Saul. (1 Samuel 10:1)
5. Because Saul rejected the word of the LORD. (1 Samuel 15:23)
6. Samuel anointed David as the second king of Israel. (1 Samuel 16:13)
7. Saul was afraid of David because the LORD was with David but had left Saul. (1 Samuel 18:12)
8. David crept up unnoticed and cut off the skirt of Saul's robe. (1 Samuel 24:4)
9. Abigail. (1 Samuel 25:32-33)
10. Saul's life ends when he took his own sword and fell on it. (1 Samuel 31:3-4)

Answers for Week 13 – 2 Samuel Chapters 1-24

1. They mourned, wept, and fasted till evening for Saul. (2 Samuel 1:12)
2. His nurse picked him up and fled, but as she hurried to leave, he fell and became crippled. His name was Mephibosheth. (2 Samuel 4:4)
3. Uzzah was struck down by God and died when he reached out and took hold of the ark of God. (2 Samuel 6:6-7)
4. David should have been out to battle with his servants. (2 Samuel 11:1)

Answers

5. David tried to trick Uriah because he had impregnated Uriah's wife. It didn't work because Uriah was faithful to his king and slept at the entrance to the palace, not with his wife. (2 Samuel 11:8-11)

6. Uriah was put on the front line of battle, and he died. (2 Samuel 11:14-17)

7. The LORD struck the child and he became ill. On the seventh day the child died. (2 Samuel 12:15-18)

8. Solomon. (2 Samuel 12:24)

9. Absalom ordered his men to kill Amnon. (2 Samuel 13:28)

10. To overthrow the kingdom of his father, David. (2 Samuel 15:1-13)

11. Absalom died after Joab thrust three darts in his heart, and 10 young men smote and slew him. (2 Samuel 18:14-15)

Answers for Week 14 – 1 Kings Chapters 1-22

1. Adonijah. (1 Kings 1:5)
2. Solomon. (1 Kings 1:30)
3. David reigned 40 years. (1 Kings 2:11)
4. Wisdom. (1 Kings 3:9)
5. David was a man of war, and Solomon was a man of peace. (1 Kings 5:3-5)
6. The temple was finished in seven years. (1 Kings 6:38) It took Solomon thirteen years to build his palace. (1 Kings 7:1)
7. Queen of Sheba. (1 Kings 10:1)
8. Solomon had 700 wives and 300 concubines. His wives turned his heart after other gods. (1 Kings 11:3-4)
9. Ahab did more evil in the eyes of the LORD, and he married Jezebel. (1 Kings 16:30-31)
10. 850. (1 Kings 18:19)
11. Elijah threw his cloak around Elisha. (1 Kings 19:19)
12. He reigned two years over Israel because he worshipped Baal, and did evil in the sight of the LORD. (1Kings 22:51-53)

Journey Through the Bible in Eleven Months

Answers for Week 15 – 2 Kings Chapters 1-25

1. Elijah did not die. A chariot of fire and horses of fire appeared, and he went by a whirlwind into heaven. (2 Kings 2:11)
2. Elijah told the poor widow to go and ask all her neighbors for empty jars. Those jars were filled by just a little oil. She was able to pay off her husband's debt. (2 Kings 4:1-7)
3. The LORD opened the servants' eyes, and he saw the mountain full of horses and chariots of fire all around Elisha. (2 Kings 6:17)
4. Jehu, king of Israel, appointed by Elisha. (2 Kings 9:1-10, 21)
5. Jezebel was thrown out of the window and eaten by dogs. (2 Kings 9:32-37)
6. The Assyrians. (2 Kings 17:18-23)
7. King Hezekiah. (2 Kings 18:3-6)
8. He added 15 years to Hezekiah's life. (2 Kings 20:6)
9. Josiah. (2 Kings 22:1, 23:25)

Answers for Week 16 – 1 Chronicles Chapters 1-29

1. Adam. (1 Chronicles 1:1)
2. Noah, Shem, Ham, and Japhet, and all of their wives. (1 Chronicles 1:4)
3. Reuben, Simeon, Levi, Judah, Dan, Naphtali, Gad, Asher, Issachar, Zebulun, Joseph, and Benjamin. (1 Chronicles 2:1-2)
4. Saul died because of his transgression against the LORD, and for consulting a medium for guidance. (1 Chronicles 10:13-14)
5. The Levites may carry the ark of God because the LORD chose them. (1 Chronicles 15:2)
6. David gave a loaf of bread, a good piece of flesh, and a flagon of wine to each Israelite man and woman. (1 Chronicles 16:3)
7. The consequences were 70,000 men of Israel fell dead. (1 Chronicles 21:1-14)
8. David's son Solomon. (1 Chronicles 23:1)

Answers

9. The Levites were priests who were to supervise the work of the temple, to be officers and judges, porters, and to praise the LORD with musical instruments. (1 Chronicles 23:4-5)
10. Because David had been a man of war and had shed blood. (1 Chronicles 28:3)

Answers for Week 17 – 2 Chronicles Chapters 1-18

1. God gave Solomon wisdom, knowledge, riches, wealth, and honor. (2 Chronicles 1:12)
2. In Jerusalem on mount Moriah. (2 Chronicles 3:1)
3. The most holy place. (2 Chronicles 5: 7)
4. God told the people to humble themselves, pray, seek His face, and turn from their wicked ways. (2 Chronicles 7:14)
5. The Queen of Sheba came to Jerusalem to test Solomon with hard questions. (2 Chronicles 9:1)
6. 40 years. (2 Chronicles 9:30)
7. Asa did what was good and right in the eyes of the LORD his God. (2 Chronicles 14:2)
8. Azariah encouraged Asa by saying the LORD is with you while you be with Him, and not let your hands be weak for your work shall be rewarded. (2 Chronicles 15:2,7)

Answers for Week 18 – 2 Chronicles Chapters 19-36

1. Jehoram slew all his brothers with a sword. (2 Chronicles 21:4)
2. He married a daughter of Ahab. (2 Chronicles 21:6)
3. Amaziah brought back the gods of the people of Seir (heathens), set them up, and bowed down to them and burned sacrifices to them. (2 Chronicles 25:14)
4. Uzziah's pride led to his downfall. He was unfaithful to the LORD. Uzziah took it upon himself to act like a priest. The LORD afflicted him with leprosy until the day he died. (2 Chronicles 26:16-21)
5. Jotham grew powerful because he prepared his ways before the LORD his God. (2 Chronicles 27:6)
6. Hezekiah was 25 years old when he began to reign, and he did that which was right in the sight of the LORD. (2 Chronicles 29:1-2)

Journey Through the Bible in Eleven Months

7. Sennacherib was killed by his own sons. (2 Chronicles 32:20-21)
8. Josiah was 16 years old when he began to seek the LORD. (2 Chronicles 34:3)
9. Jehoiakim. (2 Chronicles 36:5)
10. 70 years. (2 Chronicles 36:21)

Answers for Week 19 – Ezra Chapters 1-10

1. In the second month of the second year. (Ezra 3:8)
2. The Levites. (Ezra 3:9)
3. Ezra was a priest and a scribe of the law. (Ezra 7:12-13)
4. The people of Israel have not kept themselves separate from the neighboring peoples with their abominations and have mingled the holy race with the people around them. (Ezra 9:1-2)

Answers for Week 19 – Nehemiah Chapters 1-13

1. He was the King's cupbearer. (Nehemiah 1:11)
2. To be sent to Judah so that he can rebuild it (the walls). (Nehemiah 2:5)
3. Sanballat, Tobiah, and Geshem. First they mocked him, tried to harm him, tried to frighten him, and tried to trick him with his own people. (Nehemiah 2:19; 6:2-14)
4. For God to remember him with favor. (Nehemiah 5:19)
5. 52 days. (Nehemiah 6:15)
6. They had not met the Israelites with bread and water but had hired Balaam to curse them. (Nehemiah 13:2)
7. Remember me, O my God, for good. (Nehemiah 13:31)

Answers for Week 20 – Esther Chapters 1-10

1. Because Queen Vashti refused to come when summoned. (Esther 1:10-19)
2. Mordecai, her cousin, and her Jewish name was Hadassah. (Esther 2:7)
3. Haman was enraged that Mordecai would not bow down to him (he wanted to destroy all the Jews because he knew that they would only give reverence to the Almighty God). (Esther 3:5-6)

Answers

4. And who knows but that you have come to royal position for such a time as this. (Esther 4:14)

5. Haman was made to honor Mordecai by adorning him with the King's apparel and brought him through the city on the King's horse, and proclaiming before him, thus shall be done unto the man whom the king delighteth to honor. (Esther 6:6-7:6)

6. They hanged Haman and his 10 sons on the gallows. (Esther 7:10; 9:13)

7. Purim. (Esther 9:28)

Answers for Week 20 – Job Chapters 1-17

1. Job was perfect and upright, one who feared God, and eschewed evil. He had seven sons and three daughters. (Job 1:1-2)

2. Satan. (Job 1:6)

3. Satan was not to put his hand on Job. (Job 1:12)

4. Job got up, rent his mantle, shaved his head, fell down on the ground, and worshipped. And said, Naked came I out of my mother's womb, and naked shall I return thither: the LORD gave, and the LORD hath taken away; blessed be the name of the LORD. (Job 1:20-21)

5. Job told her she spoke as a foolish woman. (Job 2:10)

6. Seven days and seven nights. (Job 2:13)

7. He cursed the day of his birth. (Job 3:1-3)

8. Your children have sinned against you and God has cast them away because of their transgression. (Job 8:4)

9. Job keeps insisting that he is not wicked. (Job 10:7)

10. Job's plea was to speak to and argue his case with God. (Job 13:3)

11. They were miserable comforters. (Job 16:2)

Answers for Week 21 – Job Chapters 18-42

1. There are many answers to this question. Bildad: Surely such are the dwelling of the wicked; and this is the place of him that knoweth not God. Job: (Job 18:21) (Job) Have pity upon me, have pity upon me, O ye my friends; for the hand of God hath touched me.

Journey Through the Bible in Eleven Months

(Job 19:21) (Zophar) because he hath oppressed and hath forsaken the poor; because he hath violently taken away an house which he builded not. (Job 20:19) (Job) How then comfort ye me in vain, seeing in your answers there remaineth falsehood. (Job 21:34) (Eliphaz) Is not thy wickedness great? And thine iniquities infinite? (Job 22:5) (Job) But he knoweth the way that I take; When he hath tried me, I shall come forth as gold. (Job 23:10)

2. Job states his lips will not speak wickedness, and he will remain righteous before the LORD as long as he lives. (Job 27:3-6)
3. God speaks from the whirlwind. (Job 38:1)
4. Job decides he is not worthy to answer the LORD's questions. (Job 40:3-5)
5. Wherefore I abhor myself, and repent in dust and ashes. (Job 42:1-6)
6. God told Job's friends to take seven bullocks and seven rams to Job and offer up for themselves a burnt offering. (Job 42:8)
7. His brothers, sisters, and friends ate bread with him, bemoaned him, comforted him, gave him a piece of money, and an earring of gold. (Job 42:11)
8. By blessing him with 14,000 sheep, 6,000 camels, 1,000 yoke of oxen, 1,000 she asses, seven sons, and three daughters. (Job 42:12-13)

Answers for Week 22 – Psalms Numbers 1-25

1. His delight is in the law of the LORD. (Psalm 1:2)
2. The LORD has set apart the godly for Himself. (Psalm 4:3)
3. The psalmist wants the LORD to hear his voice in the morning. (Psalm 5:3)
4. The LORD has heard the voice of his weeping, supplication, and prayer. (Psalm 6:8-9)
5. David's shield is God most high, who saves the upright in heart. (Psalm 7:10)
6. Them that seek the LORD. (Psalm 9:10)
7. On the wicked, God will rain snares, fire and brimstone, and a horrible storm. (Psalm 11:6)
8. The fool has said in his heart, there is no God. (Psalm 14:1)
9. By being faithful, blameless, and pure. (Psalm 18:25-26)

Answers

10. He who has clean hands, a pure heart, and has not lifted his soul unto vanity, nor has sworn deceitfully. (Psalm 24:4)

Answers for Week 23 – Psalms Numbers 26-50

1. David asks to dwell in the house of the LORD all the days of his life. (Psalm 27:4)
2. God's anger lasts a moment; His favor lasts for life. (Psalm 30:5)
3. God has stored up His goodness. (Psalm 31:19)
4. God gives them the desires of their heart. (Psalm 37:4)
5. David's thirst and joy is for the living God. (Psalm 42:2)
6. To know that I am God. (Psalm 46:10)
7. All reasonable answers are acceptable.

Answers for Week 24 – Psalms Numbers 51-75

1. David sinned and did evil in God's sight. (Psalm 51:4)
2. The fool says in his heart there is no God. (Psalm 53:1)
3. His mercy reaches to the heavens, and His truth reaches to the clouds. (Psalm 57:10)
4. David asks God to lead him to the rock that is higher than him. (Psalm 61:2)
5. All the earth. (Psalm 66:1)
6. From his youth. (Psalm 71:5)
7. Dregs. (Psalm 75:8)

Answers for Week 25 – Psalms Numbers 76-100

1. The voice of God's thunder is in the heaven, the lightnings lightened the world, and the earth trembled and shook. (Psalm 77:18)
2. Psalm 78 is the history of the children of Israel, from the time of the Exodus from Egypt, till the time of David. God blessed, but the people sinned. God became angry, the people repented.
3. God will not withhold any good thing from them. (Psalm 84:11)
4. Psalm 91 has no wrong answer, as long as you see that our God loves you.
5. Their end is that God will cut them off. (Psalm 94)

Journey Through the Bible in Eleven Months

6. The people of God will serve Him with gladness; come before His presence with singing, enter into His gates with thanksgiving, and enter into His courts with praise, and be thankful unto Him and bless His name. Because the LORD is good, His mercy is everlasting, and His truth endureth to all generations. (Psalm 100)

Answers for Week 26 – Psalms Numbers 101-125

1. The faithful will dwell with the LORD, and He will cut off all wicked doers from His city. (Psalm 101:6-8)
2. Any answers from this Psalm are acceptable. (Psalm 103)
3. Abraham, Isaac, Jacob, Joseph, Moses, and Aaron. Answers will vary about what you may know about each one of them. (Psalm 105)
4. The fear of the LORD is the beginning of wisdom. (Psalm 111:10)
5. Psalm 117 is the shortest Psalm with two verses. (Psalm 117)
6. Psalm 119 is the longest Psalm with 176 verses. (Psalm 119)
7. To those that be good, and who are upright in heart. (Psalm 125:4)

Answers for Week 27 – Psalms Numbers 126-150

1. They were like men who dreamed. (Psalm 126:1)
2. The oath was that if David's children kept God's covenant and testimony, then his children's children will sit upon David's throne for evermore. (Psalm132:11-12)
3. The idols of the heathen are silver and gold, they have mouths, but cannot speak, eyes, but cannot see, ears, but cannot hear, nor is there breath in their mouths. (Psalm 135:15-17)
4. The theme of Psalm 136 is to give God thanks for His goodness and mercy. (Psalm 136)
5. The psalmist is going to praise God every day for ever and ever. (Psalm 145:2)
6. They all start and end with Praise ye the LORD. (Psalm 146-150)

Extra Credit Answer: Psalm 90 and Moses wrote it.

Answers for Week 28 – Proverbs Chapters 1-31

1. Solomon. For obtaining wisdom, instruction, and understanding. (Proverbs 1:1-4)

Answers

2. We are to look for it as silver and search for it as for hidden treasure. (Proverbs 2:4)

3. Because the LORD disciplines those He loves. (Proverbs 3:12)

4. The way of the wicked is like darkness. (Proverbs 4:19)

5. The strange woman uses her words to entice, her end is bitter, her feet go to death. (Proverbs 5:3-5)

6. Wisdom was brought forth, from the beginning, before the earth ever was. (Proverbs 8:22-31)

7. He, who spares the rod, hates his son. (Proverbs 13:24)

8. The name of the LORD is a strong tower. (Proverbs 18:10)

9. The candle of the LORD searches the inward heart of man. (Proverbs 20:27)

10. He who loves a pure heart and has gracious speech. (Proverbs 22:11)

11. Give our enemy bread to eat and water to drink because the LORD will reward us. (Proverbs 25:21-22)

12. The virtuous woman. (Proverbs 31:10-31)

Answers for Week 29 – Ecclesiastes Chapters 1-12

1. Solomon. (Ecclesiastes 1:1)

2. Grief and sorrow. (Ecclesiastes 1:13-18)

3. Not being remembered. (Ecclesiastes 2:16)

4. To everything there is season and a time to every purpose under the heaven. (Ecclesiastes 3:1)

5. In the place of judgment was wickedness, and in the place of righteousness, iniquity was there. (Ecclesiastes 3:16-17)

6. A vow to God is serious because He has no pleasure in fools. (Ecclesiastes 5:4-5)

7. A good name is better than perfume and the day of death better than the day of birth. (Ecclesiastes 7:1)

8. The conclusion of the whole matter is to fear God and keep His commandments. (Ecclesiastes 12:13)

Journey Through the Bible in Eleven Months

Answers to Week 29 – Song of Solomon Chapters 1-8

1. I am black, but comely. (Song of Solomon 1:5)
2. Rise up my love, my fair one, and come away. (Song of Solomon 2:10-11)
3. She stole his heart with one glance of her eyes. (Song of Solomon 4:9)
4. Place me like a seal over your heart, like a seal on your arm. (Song of Solomon 8:6)

Answers for Week 30 – Isaiah Chapters 1-33

1. God says to bring no more vain offerings and incense to Him. His soul hates the new moons and appointed feasts for they are a burden to Him and He is weary of bearing them. (Isaiah 1:13-14)
2. They will be humbled (brought low). (Isaiah 2:12)
3. The vineyard of the LORD is the house of Israel. He saw oppression and heard a cry. (Isaiah 5:7)
4. Here am I, send me. (Isaiah 6:8)
5. The sign is a virgin will conceive, bear a son, and call his name Immanuel. (Isaiah 7:14)
6. The prophesy is God's light will shine on them. (Isaiah 9:2)
7. (Isaiah 9:6)
8. The root of Jesse is Jesus, and He shall stand for an ensign (sign) for the people; to it shall the Gentiles seek: and His rest shall be glorious (Isaiah 11:10)
9. Judgment on the heathen nations for their treatment of God's people. (Isaiah 13-23)
10. The morning star is Lucifer, and he will make himself like the Most High. He shall be brought down to hell, to the sides of the pit. (Isaiah 14:12-17)
11. The work of righteousness is peace, and the effect of righteousness is quietness and assurance for ever. (Isaiah 32:17)

Answers for Week 31 – Isaiah Chapters 34-66

1. He was told to say be strong, fear not, your God will come with vengeance, and He will come to save you. (Isaiah 35: 4)
2. In the 14th year of King Hezekiah's reign. (Isaiah 36:1)
3. 185,000. (Isaiah 37:36)

Answers

4. Hezekiah showed them all the treasures that was in his house. (Isaiah 39:2)

5. The consequences were that all the treasures in his house will be carried off to Babylon. (Isaiah 39:6)

6. Isaiah says that they will renew their strength, mount up with wings as eagles, they shall run and not be weary, and they shall walk and not faint. (Isaiah 40:31)

7. When you pass through the waters, I will be with you, when you pass through the rivers, they will not sweep over you, and when you walk through the fire, you will not be burned. (Isaiah 43:2)

8. Chapter 53 is about Jesus Christ who has no form or comeliness, and when we see Him there is no beauty that we should desire Him. (Isaiah 53:2)

9. God revealed Himself to those who did not ask for Him; found by those that did not seek Him, and to a nation that did not call on His name. (Isaiah 65:1)

Extra Credit Answer: Isaiah is a major prophet because of the length of his prophesies.

Answers for Week 32 – Jeremiah Chapters 1-31

1. King Josiah. God said to Jeremiah before he was formed in the belly He knew Him, and before he came forth out of the womb He sanctified Him, and He ordained him a prophet unto the nations. (Jeremiah 1:2-5)

2. God's wrath will come forth like fire, and burn that none can quench it. (Jeremiah 4:4)

3. Jeremiah was trying to find any man that executes judgment and seeks the truth, then God will forgive this city. (Jeremiah 5:1)

4. The prophets prophesy falsely, the priests rule by their own authority, and the people love it this way. (Jeremiah 5:31)

5. From the least to the greatest, all are greedy for gain; from the prophets to the priests, all practice deceit. (Jeremiah 6:13)

6. Five of the Ten Commandments were being broken–stealing, murder, adultery, lying, and serving other gods. (Jeremiah 7:9)

Journey Through the Bible in Eleven Months

7. Let not the wise man glory (boast) of his wisdom, or the mighty man glory (boast) of his strength, or the rich man glory (boast) of his riches. (Jeremiah 9:23)
8. Jeremiah should not marry and have sons or daughters in Jerusalem. (Jeremiah 16:2)
9. Both prophet and priest are profane and wicked. (Jeremiah 23:11)
10. The king of Babylon was Nebuchadnezzar. (Jeremiah 25:1)
11. Jeremiah said the whole land will become a desolate wasteland and their captivity will last 70 years. (Jeremiah 25:11)
12. They were put to death for prophesying a lie in the LORD's name. (Jeremiah 29:21)

Answers for Week 33 – Jeremiah Chapters 32-52

1. The king cut the scroll with a penknife and cast it into the fire. (Jeremiah 36:23)
2. The king of Babylon put out Zedekiah's eyes, bound him in chains, and took him to Babylon. (Jeremiah 39:7)
3. They wanted God to show them the way they should walk, and the thing that they may do. (Jeremiah 42:3)
4. Because Jeremiah knew if they went to Egypt, they would die by the sword, famine, and pestilence. (Jeremiah 42:22)
5. When Nebuchadnezzar comes he shall smite the land of Egypt by bringing death to those destined for death, captivity to those destined for captivity, and the sword to those destined for the sword. (Jeremiah 43:11)
6. Edom shall be a desolation like Sodom and Gomorrah, and no one will live there. (Jeremiah 49:17-18)
7. There was a total of 4,600 Jews taken into captivity. (Jeremiah 52:28-30)

Answers for Week 33 – Lamentations Chapters 1-5

1. The writer describes this once full city as deserted, as a widow that was once great among the nations, and once a princess, now a slave. (Lamentations 1:1)
2. The writer weeps because there is no one to comfort him. (Lamentations 1:16)
3. The nation is not completely destroyed or consumed because of the LORD's mercies and his compassion shall fail not. (Lamentations 3:21-25)

Answers

Extra Credit Answer 1: Lamentations means to cry out loud.

Extra Credit Answer 2: Jeremiah whose nickname is the weeping prophet.

Extra Credit Answer 3: Examples: sad, devastating, heartbreaking, etc.

Answers for Week 34 – Ezekiel Chapters 1-30

1. Ezekiel was a priest. (Ezekiel 1:3)
2. God addresses Ezekiel as son of man. (Ezekiel 2:1)
3. The left side was 390 days for the house of Israel, and the right side was 40 days for the house of Judah. These days represented the number of years of their iniquity. (Ezekiel 4:5-6)
4. To go throughout the city of Jerusalem and put a mark on the foreheads of those who cry over all the detestable things that are done there. (Ezekiel 9:4)
5. The first face, a cherub; the second face, a man; the third face, a lion, and the fourth face, an eagle. (Ezekiel 10:14)
6. Because of the sins he has committed his righteousness shall not be mentioned, and he will die in his sin. (Ezekiel 18:24)
7. If a wicked man turns away from his wickedness, he will save his life. (Ezekiel 18:27)
8. The metals are brass, tin, iron, and lead which have been left in the furnace too long, and have become dross (worthless) of silver. (Ezekiel 22:18)
9. In the midst of the furnace to be melted. (Ezekiel 22:20)
10. In the ninth year, in the 10th month, and on the 10th day. (Ezekiel 24:1)
11. His wife and he was not to mourn, nor weep, nor cry. (Ezekiel 24:16-18)
12. He seems to be speaking to Satan. (See Ezekiel 28:12-19 for verses of proof)

Journey Through the Bible in Eleven Months

Answers for Week 35 – Ezekiel Chapters 31-48

1. Those who took the warning, their souls were saved, and those who did not take the warning, their blood was upon them. (Ezekiel 33:5)
2. The valley was full of dry bones. (Ezekiel 37:1-2)
3. Ezekiel saw the glory of the LORD come from the east gate. (Ezekiel 43:2)
4. The House of Israel was to observe the Passover in the first month on the 14th day, and it was to last for seven days. (Ezekiel 45:21)

Answers for Week 35 – Daniel Chapters 1-12

1. The chief official gave them new names: to Daniel, the name Belteshazzar; to Hananiah, Shadrach; to Mishael, Meshach; and to Azariah, Abednego. (Daniel 1:7)
2. To Daniel and his three friends God gave knowledge and skill in all learning and wisdom, and to Daniel he also gave understanding in all visions and dreams. (Daniel 1:17)
3. Nebuchadnezzar shouted for them to come out and come to him. (Daniel 3:25-26)
4. King Nebuchadnezzar. (Daniel 4:18-22)
5. When he saw fingers of a man's hand come forth and write upon the plaster of the wall. (Daniel 5:5-6)
6. Daniel was saved by God sending an angel who shut the lions' mouths. (Daniel 6:22)
7. Judgment is taking place. (Daniel 7:9-10)
8. Because the prince of the Persian kingdom resisted him. (Daniel 10:5; 11-13)

Answers for Week 36 – Hosea Chapters 1-14

1. Gomer. (Hosea 1:3)
2. Hosea bought her back for 15 pieces of silver and a homer and a half of barley. Hosea told Gomer that she would abide with him for many days, not play the harlot, and not be for another man. (Hosea 3:2)
3. The charge of cursing, lying, murder, stealing, and committing adultery. (Hosea 4:2)
4. The spirit of whoredom. (Hosea 5:4)

Answers

5. God desires mercy and acknowledgment of Him. (Hosea 6:6)

6. God hated them. (Hosea 9:15)

7. God will heal their backsliding, love them freely, and turn His anger away from them. (Hosea 14:4)

Answers for Week 36 – Joel Chapters 1-3

1. Palmerworm, locust, cankerworm, and caterpillar. (Joel 1:4)

2. Because the new wine will be cut off from their mouths. (Joel 1:5-6)

3. Your sons and daughters will prophesy, your old men will dream dreams, and your young men will see visions. (Joel 2:28)

4. Whosoever shall call on the name of LORD will be saved. (Joel 2:32)

5. The valley of Jehoshaphat is where all the heathen will be judged. (Joel 3:12)

Answers for Week 36 – Amos Chapters 1-9

1. Amos was a herdsman of Tekoa. (Amos 1:1)

2. The children of Israel and all their iniquities. (Amos 3:1-2)

3. Seek the LORD and live. (Amos 5:6)

4. The day of the LORD will be darkness. (Amos 5:20)

5. The famine of hearing the words of the LORD. (Amos 8:11)

Answers for Week 37 – Obadiah Chapter 1

1. Because of the violence done against his brother, Jacob, shame shall cover Edom, and he shall be cut off forever (no longer exists as a nation). (Obadiah 1:10)

Answers for Week 37 – Jonah Chapters 1-4

1. The city of Nineveh because of its wickedness. (Jonah 1:2)

2. Because Jonah felt it was his fault the great storm had come upon them. (Jonah 1:12)

3. Because Jonah was swallowed by a great fish. (Jonah 1:17)

4. The Ninevites believed God, proclaimed a fast, put on sackcloth, and turned from their evil ways. (Jonah 3:5, 10)

Journey Through the Bible in Eleven Months

5. Because the Ninevites turned from their evil ways, and God did not punish them as He said He would. (Jonah 3:10-4:2)

Answers for Week 37 – Micah Chapters 1-7

1. The mountains melt beneath Him and the valleys split apart, like wax before the fire, like water rushing down a slope. (Micah 1:3-4)
2. The leaders judge for a bribe, the priests teach for a price, and the prophets tell fortunes for money. (Micah 3:11)
3. Bethlehem Ephratah. (Micah 5:2)
4. God has shown them what is good, and He requires them to do justly, to love mercy, and to walk humbly with Him. (Micah 6:8)
5. Because a son dishonors his father, a daughter rises up against her mother, a daughter-in-law against her mother-in-law. (Micah 7:6)

Answers for Week 37 – Nahum Chapters 1-3

1. Nineveh. (Nahum 1:1)
2. The LORD cares for those that trust in Him, and darkness shall pursue His enemies. (Nahum 1:7-8)
3. It is said that your shepherds slumber, your nobles dwell in the dust, your people will scatter on the mountains with no one to gather them, and nothing can heal them. (Nahum 3:18-19)

Answers for Week 37 – Habakkuk Chapters 1-3

1. How long shall I cry, and You will not hear? Why won't You not save me from violence? Why do You show me iniquity and behold grievance? Because destruction and violence were before him. (Habakkuk 1:2-4)
2. The vision is waiting for an appointed time. (Habakkuk 2:3)
3. His belly trembled, his lips quivered, decay entered into his bones, and he shook within himself. (Habakkuk 3:16)

Answers

Answers for Week 37 – Zephaniah Chapters 1-3

1. Zephaniah's great-great grandfather was Hezekiah. (Zephaniah 1:1)
2. That day will be a day of wrath, a day of distress and anguish, a day of trouble and ruin, a day of darkness and gloominess, a day of clouds and thick darkness, a day of trumpet and battle. (Zephaniah 1:15-16)
3. He says to the meek to seek righteousness and seek meekness, so they may be hid in the day of the LORD's anger. (Zephaniah 2:3)
4. Her princes are roaring lions. Her judges are evening wolves. Her prophets are light and treacherous persons. Her priests have polluted the sanctuary, and have done violence to the law. (Zephaniah 3:3-4)

Answers for Week 37 – Haggai Chapters 1-2

1. To let the people know it's time to build God's house. (Haggai 1:8)
2. The present house of the LORD is greater than the former house, and in this place He will give peace. (Haggai 2:9)

Answers for Week 38 – Zechariah Chapters 1-14

1. They walked to and fro throughout the earth. (Zechariah 1:8-11)
2. If Joshua walked in the LORD's ways, and kept His charge (covenants), then he would judge the LORD's house, have charge of His courts, and be given a place. (Zechariah 3:6-7)
3. This is wickedness. (Zechariah 5:7-8)
4. The chariots represent the four spirits (winds) of the heavens, and they go forth from standing before the LORD of all the earth. (Zechariah 6:5)
5. The lowly king comes riding on a donkey, on a colt, the foal of a donkey. (Zechariah 9:9)
6. The LORD will bring them through the fire and will refine them as silver is refined, and will try them as gold is tried. (Zechariah 13:8-9)

Journey Through the Bible in Eleven Months

Answers for Week 38 – Malachi Chapters 1-4

1. The LORD said he loved Jacob, and hated Esau. (Malachi 1:2-3)
2. The priests offered polluted bread upon God's altar. (Malachi 1:7)
3. In tithes and offerings. Bring God your tithes. (Malachi 3:8-10)
4. The Prophet Elijah. (Malachi 4:5)

Answers for Week 38 – Mathew Chapters 1-10

1. 42 generations. (Matthew 1:17)
2. Gold, frankincense, and myrrh. (Matthew 2:11)
3. John, the Baptist; this is my beloved son in whom I am well pleased. (Matthew 3:13-17)
4. Two brothers, Simon (Peter), and Andrew, his brother. (Matthew 4:18)
5. The pure in heart shall see God, and the peacemakers shall be called the children of God. (Matthew 5:8-9)
6. The gate that leads to destruction is wide, and the gate that leads to life is narrow. (Matthew 7:13-14)
7. Jesus gave them power against unclean spirits, to cast them out, and to heal all manner of sickness and all manner of disease. (Matthew 10:1)

Answers for Week 39 – Matthew Chapters 11-28

1. Blasphemy against the Holy Spirit will not be forgiven. (Matthew 12:31)
2. Jesus says that by your words you will either be justified or condemned. (Matthew 12:36-37)
3. A prophet is not without honor except in his own country and his own house. (Matthew 13:57)
4. John was beheaded while he was in the prison. (Matthew 14:10)
5. About 5,000 men, besides women and children. (Matthew 14:21)
6. Jesus healed the Canaanite woman's daughter because of the woman's great faith. (Matthew 15:28)
7. The matters of the law are judgment, mercy, and faith. (Matthew 23:23)
8. Here are three signs: famines, pestilences, and earthquakes. (Matthew 24:4-14)

Answers

9. "O my Father, if it be possible, let this cup pass from me: nevertheless not as I will, but as thou wilt." (Matthew 26:39)

10. His wife's message was to not have anything to do with that innocent (just) man. (Matthew 27:19)

Answers for Week 39 – Mark Chapters 1-8

1. Because the demons knew who Jesus was. (Mark 1:34)

2. Jesus said, "I came not to call the righteous, but sinners to repentance." (Mark 2:17)

3. Those who do God's will is my brother, sister, and mother. (Mark 3:35)

4. Jesus said, "TALITHA CUMI; (which is being interpreted) Damsel (I say unto thee) arise." (Mark 5:41)

5. Jesus was referring to what comes out of a man's heart: adulteries, fornication, murders, thefts, covetousness, wickedness, deceit, lasciviousness, an evil eye, blasphemy, pride, and foolishness. (Mark 7:20-23)

Answers for Week 40 – Mark Chapters 9-16

1. Jesus said, "It is easier for a camel to go through the eye of a needle than for a rich man to enter into the kingdom of God." (Mark 10:25)

2. Hosanna, blessed is He who comes in the name of the Lord. Blessed is the coming kingdom of our father David. Hosanna in the highest. (Mark 11:9-10)

3. The first commandment is "Hear, O Israel; The Lord our God is one Lord: And thou shalt love the Lord thy God with all thy heart, and with all thy soul, and with all thy mind, and with all thy strength." (Mark 12:29-30)

4. For the elect's sake whom He has chosen. (Mark 13:19-20)

5. That Judas will give Jesus a kiss. (Mark 14:44)

6. Simon, a Cyrenian. (Mark 15:21)

7. Jesus cried out, "ELOI, ELOI, LAMA SABACHTHANI?" which means "My God, My God, why hast thou forsaken me?" (Mark 15:34)

8. Joseph of Arimathea. (Mark 15:43)

Journey Through the Bible in Eleven Months

Answers for Week 40 – Luke Chapters 1-20

1. The angel stated he was Gabriel who stood in the presence of God, and was sent to tell Zechariah the good news. (Luke 1:19)
2. The baby leaped in her womb, and Elisabeth said that Mary was blessed among women, and blessed is the child she will bear. (Luke 1:41-42)
3. John answered them by saying that he baptized them with water, but one mightier than him comes whose shoes he is not worthy to unloose. (Luke 3:15-16)
4. Jesus replied, "Go your way, and tell John what things ye have seen and heard; how that the blind see, the lame walk, the lepers are cleansed, the deaf hear, the dead are raised, to the poor the gospel is preached." (Luke 7:22)
5. Legion. (Luke 8:30)
6. Every kingdom divided against itself will be ruined, and a house divided against itself will fall. (Luke 11:17)
7. There is joy in the presence of the angels of God because of a sinner that repents. (Luke 15:10)
8. We are to receive it as a little child. (Luke 18:17)

Answers for Week 41 – Luke Chapters 21-24

1. His prayer to the Father was to take this cup from Him; nevertheless, not His will, but His Father's will be done. (Luke 22:41-42)
2. Jesus said, "Judas, betrayest thou the son of man with a kiss?" (Luke 22:48)
3. Blasphemy. (Luke 22:70-71)
4. THIS IS THE KING OF THE JEWS. (Luke 23:38)
5. It became dark, the veil of the temple was torn in two, Jesus cried with a loud voice, "Father into thy hands I commend my spirit," then Jesus died. (Luke 23:44-46)

Answers for Week 41 – John Chapters 1-21

1. In the beginning was the Word, and the Word was with God, and the Word was God. He (Jesus) was with God in the beginning. (John 1:1-2)
2. John the Baptist came as a witness to testify concerning the Light (Jesus). (John 1:7-8)

Answers

3. Jesus was at a wedding in Cana of Galilee where He performed His first miracle of turning water into wine. (John 2:1-11)

4. God loved the world so much that He gave His only begotten son. (John 3:16)

5. In spirit and in truth. (John 4:23)

6. Jesus told the woman He is the Christ. (John 4:25-26)

7. They shall never go hungry nor thirst. (John 6:35)

8. Jesus is the Good Shepherd who gives His life for His sheep. (John 10:11)

9. Jesus wept because He was mourning the death of Lazarus. (John 11:33-35)

10. The Comforter. (John 16:7)

11. Jesus answered, "Thou couldn't have no power at all against me except it were given thee from above." (John 19:10-11)

Extra Credit Answer: (John 17)

Answers for Week 42 – Acts Chapters 1-28

1. The day of Pentecost. (Acts 2:1, 4)

2. Peter told them to repent and be baptized in the name of Jesus for remission of sins, and they will receive the gift of the Holy Spirit. (Acts 2:38)

3. Ananias and Sapphire were guilty of lying to the Holy Spirit about the price they received from the sale of their land. (Acts 5:1-10)

4. Stephen was a man full of faith and power who did great wonders and miracles among the people. He was stoned for being accused of speaking blasphemous words against Moses, God, the Holy place, and the law. His last words were, Lord, lay not this sin to their charge. (Acts 6:8-13; 7:58-60)

5. Saul was at Stephen's death and he persecuted the church. (Acts 8:1)

6. Saul was converted after being blinded on the road to Damascus when Ananias who had been sent by the Lord to restore Saul's sight, laid hands on him, and he was filled with the Holy Spirit and was baptized. (Acts 9:1-19)

7. James, the brother of John. (Acts 12:1-2)

8. Because of the contention between them they departed from each other. (Acts 15:36-39)

Journey Through the Bible in Eleven Months

9. The Bereans were very noble men who examined the scriptures for themselves to see if what Paul said was true. (Acts 17:10-11)
10. Paul was in Rome for two years, and while there he preached the kingdom of God, and taught those things which concerned the Lord Jesus Christ. (Acts 28:30-31)

Answers for Week 43 – Romans Chapters 1-16

1. Because it is the power of God for the salvation of everyone who believes. (Romans 1:16)
2. The righteousness of God which is by faith of Jesus Christ unto all and upon all them that believe. (Romans 3:21-22)
3. David said Blessed are they whose iniquities are forgiven, whose sins are covered, and Blessed is the man to whom the Lord will not impute sin. (Romans 4:6-8)
4. By the Holy Ghost. (Romans 5:5)
5. The one act of trespass was condemnation for all men, and one act of righteousness was justification of life for all men. (Romans 5:18)
6. Paul is convinced that neither death, nor life, nor angels, nor principalities, nor powers, nor things present, nor things to come, nor height, nor depth, nor any other creature shall be able to separate us from the love of God, which is Christ Jesus. (Romans 8:38-39)
7. By saying he will call them his people, which were not his people, and her beloved, which was not beloved. (Romans 9:25-26)
8. The heart has to believe unto righteousness, and the mouth has to confess unto salvation. (Romans 10:10)
9. Your reasonable service is to present your bodies as a living sacrifice, holy and acceptable unto God. (Romans 12:1)
10. To teach us that through patience and the encouragement of the scriptures we might have hope. (Romans 15:4)

Answers for Week 43 – 1 Corinthians Chapters 1-16

1. God chose the foolish things of the world to confound the wise; and God chose the weak things to confound the things which are mighty. (1 Corinthians 1:27-29)

Answers

2. When we are reviled, we bless; when we are persecuted, we suffer it, and when we are defamed, we intreat. (1 Corinthians 4:12-13)

3. A woman is free to remarry when her husband dies, only in the Lord. (1 Corinthians 7:39)

4. Paul stated he had become all things to all men so he might save some. (1 Corinthians 9:22)

5. We should all examine ourselves. (1 Corinthians 11:28)

6. Charity (love) suffers long, is kind, does not envy, is not puffed up, does not rejoice in iniquity, but rejoices in the truth. (1 Corinthians 13:4-8)

7. Death. (1 Corinthians 15:26)

Answers for Week 44 – 2 Corinthians Chapters 1-13

1. Forgive and comfort him. (2 Corinthians 2:5-8)

2. Because we are not of the letter (law), but of the spirit. (2 Corinthians 3:5-6)

3. To be judged by the things we have done in our bodies, whether good or bad. (2 Corinthians 5:10)

4. Godly sorrow produces repentance, but worldly sorrow produces death. (2 Corinthians 7:10)

5. My grace is sufficient for you: for my strength is made perfect in weakness. (2 Corinthians 12:9)

Answers for Week 44 – Galatians Chapters 1-6

1. If any man preach any other Gospel than what you have already received, let him be accursed. (Galatians 1:6-9)

2. The two different groups were the uncircumcised (Gentiles), and the circumcised (Jews). (Galatians 2:7)

3. Those who are of the faith. (Galatians 3:7)

4. The fruit of the spirit is love, joy, peace, patience, kindness, goodness, faithfulness, gentleness, and self-control. (Galatians 5:22-23)

Journey Through the Bible in Eleven Months

Answers for Week 44 – Ephesians Chapters 1-6

1. We are sealed with the Holy Spirit of promise. (Ephesians 1:13)
2. The gift of God is grace through faith. (Ephesians 2:8)
3. We are growing up in Christ. (Ephesians 4:15)
4. Husbands love your wives as Christ loves the church, and gave Himself for it because he that loves his wife, loves himself. (Ephesians 5:25; 28)
5. The full armor of God is as follows: loins girt about with truth (belt of truth), breastplate of righteousness, shoes with the preparation of the gospel of peace, shield of faith, helmet of salvation, and the sword of the spirit which is the Word of God. (Ephesians 6:13-17)

Answers for Week 44 – Philippians Chapters 1-4

1. Paul's prayer: that your love may abound yet more and more in knowledge and in all judgment; that ye may approve things that are excellent; that ye may be sincere and without offense till the day of Christ; being filled with the fruits of righteousness, which are by Jesus Christ unto the glory and praise of God. (Philippians 1:9-11)
2. What happens is their end is destruction, God is their stomach, their glory is in their shame, and they mind earthly things. (Philippians 3:18-19)
3. These things are whatever is true, whatever is noble, whatever is right, whatever is pure, whatever is lovely, whatever is of good report, whatever is virtuous, and praiseworthy. (Philippians 4:8)

Answers for Week 45 – Colossians Chapters 1-4

1. Epaphras. (Colossians 1:6-7)
2. Paul wanted their hearts to be comforted, being knit together in love, to the acknowledgment of the mystery of God, and of the Father, and of Christ; in whom are hid all the treasures of wisdom and knowledge. (Colossians 2:1-3)
3. We should teach and admonish one another through singing psalms, hymns and spiritual songs, with gratitude in our hearts to God. (Colossians 3:16)

Answers

Answers for Week 45 – 1 Thessalonians Chapters 1-3

1. Remembering without ceasing your work of faith, labor of love, and patience of hope in our Lord Jesus Christ. (1 Thessalonians 1:3)
2. To study to be quiet, to do their own business, and to work with their own hands, to win the respect of non-believers, and not have to depend on others. (1 Thessalonians 4:11-12)
3. Like a thief in the night. (1 Thessalonians 5:2)
4. In everything give thanks: for this is the will of God in Christ Jesus concerning you. (1 Thessalonians 5:18)

Answers for Week 45 – 2 Thessalonians Chapters 1-3

1. They will be punished with everlasting destruction from the presence of the Lord and from the glory of His power. (2 Thessalonians 1:9)
2. There shall be a falling away, the man of sin and destruction will be revealed, he will exalt himself and sit in the temple of God. (2 Thessalonians 2:3-4)

Answers for Week 45 – 1 Timothy Chapters 1-6

1. He wants men everywhere to pray, lifting up holy hands without wrath or disputing. (1 Timothy 2:8)
2. The qualifications are be blameless, the husband of one wife, vigilant, sober, of good behavior, given to hospitality, apt to teach; not given to wine, no striker, not greedy of filthy lucre; but patient not a brawler, not covetous; one that ruleth well his own house having his children in subjection with all gravity. (1 Timothy 3:2-7)
3. The great mystery of godliness is that God was manifest in the flesh, justified in the Spirit, seen of angels, preached unto the Gentiles, believed on in the world, and received up into glory. (1 Timothy 3:16)
4. For the love of money is the root of all evil. (1 Timothy 6:10)

Answers for Week 45 – 2 Timothy Chapters 1-4

1. A spirit of power, and of love, and of a sound mind. (2 Timothy 1:7)
2. Timothy was encouraged to study to show himself approved unto God, a workman that need not be ashamed, rightly dividing the word of truth. (2 Timothy 2:15)

Journey Through the Bible in Eleven Months

3. All scripture is inspired by God and is useful for teaching, reproof, for correction, and for instruction in righteousness. (2 Timothy 3:16)

Answers for Week 46 – Titus Chapters 1-3

1. The older women in the church are to teach the younger women to be sober, to love their husbands and children, to be discreet, chaste, keepers at home, good, and obedient to their own husbands. (Titus 2:4-5)

2. Titus was told to remind the people to be subject to principalities and authorities, to be obedient to magistrates, to be ready to every good work, to speak evil of no man, to be gentle, showing meekness unto all men. (Titus 3:1-2)

Answers for Week 46 – Philemon Chapter 1

1. Onesimus. (Philemon 1:10)

Answers for Week 46 – Hebrews Chapters 1-13

1. Another name for angels is ministering spirits who are sent to serve those who are saved. (Hebrews 1:14)

2. For the Word of God is quick and powerful and sharper than any two-edged sword, and is the discerner of the thoughts and intents of the heart. (Hebrews 4:12)

3. We are to approach the throne of God boldly, so that we may obtain mercy and find grace to help in time of need. (Hebrews 4:16)

4. He represented the high priest (Jesus) as King of righteousness, also King of Salem, which is King of peace. (Hebrews 7:1-3)

5. Jesus entered the most holy place by His own blood. (Hebrews 9:12)

6. Now faith is the substance of things hoped for, and the evidence of things not seen. (Hebrews 11:1)

7. We should lay aside every weight and the sin that so easily entangles, and let us run with patience the race that is set before us. (Hebrews 12:1)

8. We are told not to forget to entertain strangers, for by so doing some people have entertained angels without knowing it. (Hebrews 13:2)

Answers

Answers for Week 46 – James Chapters 1-5

1. We are to ask God for wisdom. (James 1:5)
2. The man is blessed who endures temptation for when he is tried, he shall receive the crown of life which the Lord has promised to them that love Him. (James 1:12)
3. The wisdom that comes from above is pure, peaceable, gentle, and easy to be entreated, full of mercy and good fruits, without partiality and without hypocrisy. (James 3:17)
4. We have saved a soul from death, and covered a multitude of sins. (James 5:20)

Answers for Week 47 – 1 Peter Chapters 1-4

1. The trial of your faith, more precious than gold, might be found unto praise, honor, and glory at the appearing of Jesus Christ. (1 Peter 1:7)
2. The eyes of the Lord are over the righteous, His ears are attentive to their prayers, but the face of the Lord is against them who do evil. (1 Peter 3:12)
3. We are to serve others as good stewards of the grace of God. (1 Peter 4:10)
4. We should humble ourselves under the mighty hand of God, that He may exalt us. (1 Peter 5:6)

Answers for Week 47 – 2 Peter Chapters 1-3

1. The promise is that if you do these things you shall never fall and will have entrance into the everlasting kingdom of our Lord and Savior Jesus Christ. (2 Peter 1:10-11)
2. Lot's righteous soul was vexed day to day by their filthy lives and unlawful ways. (2 Peter 2:7-8)
3. The heavens and earth are reserved for fire by God being kept for the day of judgment and perdition of ungodly men. (2 Peter 3:7)

Answers for Week 47 – 1 John Chapters 1-5

1. We deceive ourselves and the truth is not in us. God is faithful and just to forgive us our sins and cleanse us from all unrighteousness. (1 John 1:8-9)
2. The children of God do not commit sin, and the children of the devil are unrighteous and do not love their brothers. (1 John 3:9-10)

Answers

His throne, as Jesus sat down with His Father on His throne. (Revelation 2:7, 11, 17, 26; 3:5, 12, 21)

3. The 24 elders were clothed in white raiment, and had crowns of gold on their heads. (Revelation 4:4)

4. The first beast was like a lion, the second beast like a calf, the third beast had a face like a man, and the fourth beast like a flying eagle. They never stop saying Holy, holy, holy, Lord God Almighty, which was, and is, and is to come. (Revelation 4:6-8)

5. One of the elders told John not to weep because the lion of the tribe of Judah, the root of David, has prevailed to open the book and to loose its seven seals. (Revelation 5:4-5)

6. See Chapter 6:1-13.

7. The four angels were told not to harm the earth nor the sea until we have sealed the servants of our God in their foreheads. (Revelation 7:3)

8. When the seventh seal was opened, there was silence in heaven for about half an hour. And the seven angels were given seven trumpets. (Revelation 8:1-2)

9. Woe, woe, woe to the inhabitants of the earth, by reason of the other voices of the trumpet of the three angels, which are yet to sound. (Revelation 8:13)

10. The angel/king of the abyss's name in Hebrew is Abaddon and in Greek is Apollyon, which means destruction. (Revelation 9:11)

11. First, the scroll tasted as sweet as honey in his mouth, but when he swallowed it, his belly turned bitter. (Revelation 10:10)

12. All that dwell upon the earth whose names have not been written in the book of life belonging to the lamb. (Revelation 13:8)

13. Because the seven plagues of the seven angels were filled with the wrath of God to be poured out on the earth. (Revelation 15:8; 16:1)

14. Blessed are those who are invited to the marriage supper of the lamb. (Revelation 19:9)

15. Behold, I come quickly: Blessed is he that keepeth the sayings of the prophecy of this book. (Revelation 22:7, 12, 20)

Journey Through the Bible in Eleven Months

3. Because God's son laid down His life for us, and we should do the same for our brothers. (1 John 3:16)
4. He showed His love by sending His only begotten son into the world, that we might live through Him. (1 John 4:9-10)
5. The confidence we have in God is that if we ask anything according to His will, He hears us and we know that we have the petitions that we desired of Him. (1 John 5:14-15)

Answers for Week 47 – 2 John Chapter 1

1. John tells the elect lady and her children that we should love one another. (2 John 1:5)

Answers for Week 47 – 3 John Chapter 1

1. Because some brothers of the faith came back and testified about how Gaius continues to walk in the truth, and continues to be faithful to brothers and strangers. (3 John 1:3-5)

Answers for Week 47 – Jude Chapter 1

1. Jude is the half-brother (Matthew 13:55 and Mark 6:3) and servant of Jesus Christ and the brother of James. Jude is speaking to them that are sanctified by God the Father. (Jude 1:1)
2. He says that these men will be destroyed, and the angels that rebelled will be in everlasting chains under darkness until the day of judgment. (Jude 1:5-6)

Answers for Week 48 – Revelation Chapters 1-22

1. The book of Revelation is about Jesus Christ, and was made known to His servant John. The promise is that they will be blessed. (Revelation 1:1-3)
2. The promises to the seven churches that overcome are: 1) Ephesus: the right to eat from the tree of life, which is in the paradise of God; 2) Smyrna: will not be hurt of the second death; 3) Pergamos: some of the hidden manna, a white stone with a new name written on it; 4) Thyatira: authority over the nations; 5) Sardis: will be dressed in white, his name will not be blotted out of the book of life, but will acknowledge his name before my Father and His angels; 6) Philadelphia: make a pillar in the temple of God, and write on him the new name of God which is the new Jerusalem; 7) Laodicea: the right to sit with Jesus on

ABOUT THE AUTHOR

Carrie Carter is first and foremost a woman that loves the Lord God, the most and the best. Because of who He is and how He is in her life, she considers herself His daughter. Carrie lives in the St. Louis area and is a member of a local church, where she is active in Sunday school, Bible study, and in the food pantry. She has a large family, all of whom she loves dearly. Her passion is the study of God's Word; something she wants for all of His children. Carrie believes that to know His Word, is to know Him. Her prayer is to represent Him well.

JOURNEY THROUGH THE BIBLE IN ELEVEN MONTHS

www.ingramcontent.com/pod-product-compliance
Lightning Source LLC
Chambersburg PA
CBHW080025130526
44591CB00037B/2667